FIVE MINUTES TO COUNT

A Memoir of a Former Female Correctional Officer

BY
LISA PURTUE

Acknowledgment

I would first like to thank my spouse, James, for his unwavering support in everything I have done and accomplished since we've been together. My gratitude also extends to his father, James, and his late mother, Quintella, for their kindness and encouragement.

To all those who supported me throughout my career at various institutions, thank you for your positive influence and for fostering my growth and success. To the administrator who encouraged me to be promoted to Sergeant during my first academy training—thank you for seeing potential in me that I didn't see in myself at the time. To Captain T., I am deeply grateful for your support at the range. Your kindness and guidance helped me overcome my fear of handling a rifle and shotgun, empowering me to succeed in target training.

There are countless others who have stood by me, even during my most challenging times, including when I was a homeless teen mom. Though I cannot name everyone here, please know that your belief in me and motivation to persevere will never be forgotten.

I would also like to extend my heartfelt thanks to my Editor, Joyce White. Your encouragement and determination pushed me to publish this work, and I hope it provides women with a deeper understanding of this world. It is my belief that we must better serve people by healing those within the criminal justice system rather than retraumatizing them.

This book is just the beginning; there are many more stories to share and several volumes to follow. I hope you find this candid perspective enlightening as it offers a glimpse into the life of one female officer serving the citizens of her state and those entrusted to her care.

My journey into this service was driven by a desire to bring positive change to the lives of others—a mission I continue to uphold in every capacity I serve.

TABLE OF CONTENTS

Chapter 1
Five Minutes to Count

She looked up into the sky, smiling as the sun began to peak through the misty clouds. This fleeting glimpse would be her only sight of the morning sun, as well as her last breath of fresh air, before entering the front doors of the prison where she worked. As her eyes closed, she took that one last deep breath before opening her eyes to the harsh reality of not knowing what this day would bring after having a few days off. She continued to walk towards the front entrance reaching for the door handle. Just before grasping for the door handle, she paused, looking down at the pigeons gathered around the last bits of cookie someone left on the sidewalk wrapped in a dirty napkin, near the front entrance. Many times, she would see half-eaten food, along with wrappers, thrown on the ground as the church across the street served the poor in the area. Frequently, the people served at the church would throw the leftovers on the ground, which ended up feeding the local birds in the area. As the birds meticulously pecked at the remnants of leftover bread or cake, it reminded Officer Dean of how the so-called throwaways of our society appreciated even the little bits of kindness or gratitude, even from a single piece of bread. The church around the corner served thousands within the community who struggle every day to provide a meal for their families or even have a meal for the day. It was a sad disgusting truth.

As Officer Dean, wearing her crisp blue uniform with her two stripe patches on each side of her shirt and jacket sleeves, opened the front door to the lobby of the institution where she worked and proceeded to walk in. A very distinct smell emanated into the lobby. The image of men's sweaty gym socks or sweaty balls from a men's locker room comes to mind. A distinct smell lingered on your clothes, skin, and your emotional thoughts, especially through the hallways, the closer you came to the segregation unit. Segregation had a quite different smell depending on what the inmates were occupying their time doing. This would be another chapter. There was no central air within the building, except for the special-needs unit, so not only were the inmates affected by the heat during the summer months, but also the staff.

"Good morning, Dart! As Dean greeted the lobby officer on first shift, she walked up several flights of steps to the visitor's lobby area, where there was talk overheard about someone on a prior shift who found a small bag of weed on the steps then gave it to the captain in the lobby.

The captain on that shift apparently threw it away in the regular garbage because he couldn't prove who brought it in. As Dean threw her bag on the conveyor belt, she continued to walk through the metal half door to the other side of the conveyor belt, the alarm went off on her hair clip she had placed in her bag that morning to hold her bun in place. With the hair clip removed from her bag, with her golden blond hair well past her shoulders, she intended to fasten her hair up in a bun before heading upstairs. She grabbed her bag along with her hair clip and headed towards the captain, who did a wellness check before officers could continue to their posts. "Good morning, Captain!" she stated as she passed Captain Penny. She always had a smile, a positive attitude, and a grateful heart but received a grunt instead. That was the normal interaction given to officers by Captain Penny. He was never much for words these days since he was looking forward to retirement soon.

Captain Penny was old school and hard as nails. He had been working in the corrections field for over 30 years. He had experience working at several other facilities and was well-trusted in making good decisions, including backing most of his officers. There were always going to be exceptions to those few he did not like for whatever reason. The work he put into training new officers and running the

ERU (Emergency Response Unit) teams once a month was his pride and joy. He wanted all his officers to be safe within this dangerous environment. He often came off with a rough demeanor for good reason. He had his share of close calls involving inmates and made sure we knew it. "Tie up that hair, girl! It's for your safety!" shouted Penny. "Yes, Sir!" as Officer Dean would respond in return. She knew the rules of keeping herself safe in this environment, however, over time, she learned how to keep herself safe because she was a female in a mostly male institution.

As a female working with all male offenders, she learned by experience how to keep herself safe. She did not wear anything that had a smell, such as soap, perfume, or deodorant, and she wore her uniform loose. She was careful not to wear make-up here within this environment as it would attract attention from not only fellow officers, male or female, but especially male offenders. This was not only a dangerous environment, but female correctional staff did not want to attract attention to themselves, all for good reason. This took time to learn due to there being no classroom training for female staff about safety issues being a female correctional officer other than hostage situations and the propensity to be a hostage target.

It was a mostly male institution, a maximum at that. The institution was in the heart of a vicarious area. Not many people wanted to work there at that time. It was a very rough place to work, in fact, people were transferring to other institutions all the time. Few stayed after their six-month probationary period. The facility was a10-story high-rise institution that took approximately 10 minutes to get to the top floor if there was an emergency. Many officers ended up gaining control of their own unit before help arrived.

This Institution was no exception. With inmates who outnumbered officers 50 plus to one, it was hard to keep people working in that kind of environment. State budget cuts and the lack of pay raises took their toll on the officers who worked there. Many officers worked double shifts and were burnt out not only by the inmates who were, so to speak, in your face every day but also by the many bitter staff members. Another thing that became disheartening was to see the same inmate faces, those who just left days or a week prior, only to be locked up again. Because officers worked so much, seeing each other sometimes more than their own spouses wreaked havoc with officers' personal relationships. As with any law enforcement position, suicide, divorce, mental health issues, alcoholism, or other drug use; had been a huge issue within this line of work.

As Dean finished pinning her hair up in the staff breakroom, she then checked her mailbox for vacation slips, approved hours, or memos from the week. She grabbed her backpack and headed to her unit upstairs on the seventh floor. It took seven doors to open from control center before entering the elevator core just to get to the elevator. The elevator was full of officers, old-timers, and new officers she did not know. She was told to hide her inner shine during her probationary period; because of the many disgruntled, bitter officers who arrived at work hating their jobs and what became of their lives. In many cases, officers brought that anger to work and resented anyone who was cheerful, happy, polite, or grateful for this job. They did not understand their negative energy influenced everyone around them, including fellow staff and inmates. All she heard in that elevator was the raw epithets and frustration from those who felt they were not treated with any respect for putting their lives on the line every day, who were not even considered real law enforcement officers, but stepchildren of the law enforcement community. The old timers were discussing why they could not memorialize any fallen correctional officers at the training facility. They had to raise their own funds to create this memorial because the state budget had no money for such a project. It was a sad truth for what we did every day. The many sacrifices of our private lives for a state job took its toll on us in the form of chronic stress, trauma, broken relationships, addiction, physical and mental health problems, and our safety, but the powers to be refused to compensate for our lives being placed on the line. Anything can happen in our line of work. We expect the unexpected, every day. When the shit hit the fan, it was going down, no matter if you were ready or not.

Officer Dean could not think of a better job that was meant for her at this time of her life. It was a change from the mediocre job she had in the past, which rarely promoted women. After spending 16 years in a career field to make her father proud, it did nothing to create the bond she wanted with her dad. It was her time now to focus on a new direction and the challenge of working with people within a unique environment. She felt she was up for the challenge to bring positive change into the lives of others. After competing with 600 applicants, only 160 were accepted into the academy. The result was only 90 made it through the rigorous training over approximately two-month span of time. She was lucky enough to make it within the top ten of her class. The challenging work put into twice-daily workouts, eight hours of classroom teaching, and working within study groups prepared her for this job but not what was to come.

She thought about all the broken souls somehow ending up here at the institution. Many committed crimes by breaking the rules of their probation in some way, then were locked up, separated from those whose socially acceptable lives and resilience kept them out of such places. She felt anyone could end up behind bars as we are all one bad decision away from being here ourselves. This job was not a just a regular job anyone could work. People do not rush into a job like this. It is a job that will either make or break you mentally, physically, emotionally, and spiritually, if you let it. Sometimes she wondered if her own broken life brought her here because she could understand some of the issues at a level others could not. The perpetual stories of unemployment, homelessness, broken families, drug and alcohol addiction, childhood trauma, sexual assault/ trafficking, drug dealing, and mental illness are just some of the many areas that needed to be addressed by those who entered the institution. She believed the underlying issues, if not dealt with, could result in criminal behavior, but it does not excuse the destructive behavior issued upon helpless victims, especially children. The people who were locked up were fighting the demons within themselves, which, in many cases, were acted upon innocent people who happened to be in the vicinity. Hurt people hurt other people.

The elevator finally stopped on the seventh floor. She struggled from the back of the elevator, stating, "Hold that door open, please!" as the other officers moved to let her out into the elevator corridor. She then had to wait for control to allow her access through four other doors, then another to the inside unit corridor. Sargent Benson saw her in the corridor after hanging up the phone. He then buzzed the officer pod door open for her to enter the officer station. "Hey, guess who you'll be working with today?" stated the sergeant. "Who, Lewis?" she said as she placed her bag on the desk. "Me, just got ordered for this unit," stated the sergeant. Dean went on to say, "How lucky can I be?" stated with a smile. She liked working with Sgt. Benson. He was a great sergeant to work with. He had a great attitude and knew he could depend on Officer Dean to do a fantastic job with the inmates on this unit, or any unit. Benson used to work first shift, but due to family obligations, he took a post on third.

Unit 7B was a special unit just for diabetic inmates, and there were a lot of them. After count was cleared, each inmate who was diabetic had their cell door opened so they could come down to the medication office to be monitored and evaluated for their blood sugar levels prior to breakfast. Two inmates would come into the room at a time. Dean monitored their checks, recorded their numbers in a logbook, then issued a syringe and given their insulin, if they needed it. Some took Humalog, Lantus, or regular insulin. There was a huge risk to her if an inmate got mad. The gentlemen were now armed with a weapon, so she was always chipper, stating "Good morning!" and calling each person out by name. This meant a lot to each of the gentlemen. This also developed a positive rapport if they had serious medical issues or something else was going on.

As the two other officers were leaving for the day, Officer Dough, while handing in his keys; in return for his chit, chuckled, stated, "Hey Dean, do us a favor and inventory that lock box for us?" Dean stated, "Sure Dough, no problem!" Dough giggled as he left with his partner from third shift, Officer Stanke.

Officer Stanke and Officer Dough were placed on third shift approximately two years ago because both liked to screw with inmates. After the last incident, which was reported to upper management, Dough and Stanke told an inmate to pack up his shit because he was leaving. The inmate did just as he was told, however, both officers denied they told the inmate anything of the sort. The inmate asked all morning when intake was picking him up. Both officers stated they didn't know what was going on. This was equally upsetting for the inmate, so he started yelling at the officers to call someone soon. Eventually the officers left for the day leaving a really pissed off inmate for the next shift to deal with. The unit manager had just enough of these two clowns and referred them for discipline. Somehow both ended up on third shift working this unit.

As Dean was settling in, she saw the inmate's property box, unlocked with, what appeared to be, a white substance dripping outside of the cover. Dean looked at the box, then at Sgt. Benson, "Sgt, when was this inmate taken off the unit?" Sgt. Benson stated, "Let me look at the log, hmm… Looks like he was taken to segregation for fighting on first shift, yesterday." Sgt. Benson also looked at the box, stating, "What the hell is that shit dripping out of … Those bastards!" As Dean slipped on gloves before opening the box, she saw the inmate's property covered in lotion the inmate purchased off canteen. The empty lotion container was just thrown inside. All the inmate's legal work was covered in lotion, along with his family pictures and other personal belongings. Dean picked up the chunk of papers with lotion dripping off them as she looked at Sgt. Benson. He stated, "Could you please wipe off the lotion as best as you can, Dean?" Her response, "Sure Sgt, anything for you." Dean would have done it anyway because it was so disrespectful of what little the inmate had regarding personal property. She also didn't condone such childish behavior of fellow officers. If the officers did not like an inmate for whatever reason, they took it out on them in a personal way. As a rule, she gave respect without expecting it in return. It was our job, as officers, to keep order and not judge others, which was already done at the court level. Probation and parole had their rules they had to follow. If the inmate broke any of those rules, they ended up back here at the institution.

Well, the time was almost 0610, so Dean quickly opened the cell doors automatically from inside the officer's station, then made the morning announcement before the control sergeant broadcasted, signifying 0615 standing count. It was Dean's first day back after a four-day break, and already she was tasked with fixing the mess her fellow officers had made of an inmate's property. It looks like just another day in her life as a female correctional officer.

"GENTLEMEN, FIVE MINUTES TO COUNT"

Chapter 2
First Official Day on the Job

Officer Dean remembers her very first day at the institution after spending eight weeks at the academy with her future co-workers. Eleven new officers ended up here, including Dean. Officer Dean graduated within the top ten in her class and had the paper targets to prove it. Although the institution did not have towers, the practice of shooting a gun and overcoming the extreme fear of handling a weapon was all the reward for her.

Many years before Officer Dean entered the academy, she had a gun put to her head by an ex-boyfriend while she was carrying their child. Eight months along in her pregnancy, beaten and given black eyes by a person she trusted, only to become extremely fearful, especially of guns. Click, click, click, from the revolver placed at her temple, during an alcohol fueled and enraged situation which was sparked by her not putting a dish away which was left on the counter. This was often experienced by Dean from her ex-boyfriend and the father of her middle son. It was pure trauma which still resonated in her thoughts as she held any gun. However, years later, she slowly overcame that fear with the patience of her academy instructor,

13

Captain T., who showed her kindness on a freezing October day. She was not only shaking with fear, but the weather didn't help either. Captain T took his own jacket off and covered her with it for warmth so she could stop shaking and hit the target at 100 yards. She kept her targets from that day, which still hang in her garage as a reminder of overcoming her fear on that cold October morning and the courage to follow through with proper support. Thanks Captain T.

As Officer Dean and her co-workers were counted upon arrival at the institution, each receiving their assignment for the day in a file folder as the regular officers came into the lobby, heading to their units. One by one, some of the male officers made sexual gestures to the new female recruits, discussing openly who they were going to fuck first. This aspect of the job was not expected due to how the administrator of the academy handled a situation with three male speakers who were tasked with sharing information about gangs with the class. While in this academy training, Dean's classmates were all released on break during this class portion at the academy. Dean and another staff member overheard a conversation between these three male officers about how a female staff member became an instructor at the very academy we were in, describing how she must have given blow jobs or hand jobs to all of her superiors to get into her new position, even making hand gestures while laughing. Dean reported this behavior to the administrator, and the issues were handled immediately. Unexpectedly, the administrator called Dean into his office and asked Dean if she was interested in going straight to Sargent. Dean was very flattered; however, she declined the offer due to wanting to experience starting at the bottom just like everyone else. The professionalism displayed by this administrator at the academy cemented these expectations written by the Department of Corrections, for her.

As she waited in the lobby with the other new recruits for further instruction from her new Captain. Her thoughts were now heightened and on alert, hoping this was not what was going on here and why they needed so many new officers. Before Officer Dean accepted this job, she read a book entitled, "New Jack -Guarding Sing Sing," written by Ted Conover, from the perspective of a new correctional officer. He, in fact, was an undercover journalist who obtained a job working as a correctional officer at the infamous Sing-Sing prison in New York City. This book was an introduction to what, she felt, was what to be expected as a working officer. Not so, in fact, it was just the very tip of the iceberg of expectations or experiences Dean, and the new recruits were about to encounter. This book did not share the gory details of violent, bloody fights, sexual assaults, staff assaults, disease exposure, extreme mental health issues, serious health issues, and overall gross human behaviors that Officer Dean and others would be exposed to while working this kind of job. What this book did was give her a general overview of what HIS personal experiences as a male correctional officer were. Although everyone's experiences will be different, being a female, working with mostly all male inmates in a male-dominated field was quite another kind of experience altogether.

All new officers were called, "Slick-Sleeves or New Jacks" due to the fact they had not earned their stripes, and the inmates knew this. We were then all ushered into the central control area to go to our first assignments. As the steel doors closed behind us, silence surrounded this group. It was at this point it became very real. Then someone within the group whispered, "Mama," very quietly, making us all burst out in laughter, which was a cover for our impending doom. None of us really knew what we signed up for, however, our expectations of what the job would be like was similar to, let's make a deal. What will be behind door number two? As the next five sets of steel doors opened into an elevator core, the group had to wait again for another set of doors to open to enter the elevator. Every button was pushed, stopping at every floor. It took a while to get to each floor, and then to get out of the packed elevator was yet another story.

She went to her first unit, unit three, which was considered the special needs unit. Here, this institution holds inmates with special mental health needs. Being brand new, she didn't know what to expect. As she arrived at the officer station door, she watched the female sergeant lift her head from what appeared to be her sleeping position on her desk. She then reached over to push a button to let Dean in. As Dean entered, she stated, "Good morning, I'm Officer Dean!" The Sergeant got out of her chair and slowly walked over to Dean, invading her personal space, which she needed to back up from this person she knew nothing about. Officer Dean was now backed up against the door in which she entered, with this blond female sergeant's breasts, literally touching her crisp blue shirt. This Sargent was not a small-busted woman either. As she pressed her breasts up against Dean, moving her head back and forth, she stated, "And what y'all doin here, Barbie Doll?" The sergeant stepped back to look Dean up and down in front of two other snickering officers. It was definitely an OH SHIT moment for Dean.

It appeared the institution didn't get many Caucasian female officers willing to work there due to its location within the inner confides of this city. Dean quickly stated, "Same reason you are here, Sargent, to earn a paycheck." She then backed off as the other two officers were still contemplating what slick comment to add to the intimidation factor. Officer Dean sat down and looked at her schedule to see how long this torture would last. Damn, two hours of this, she thought.

There were approximately 30 inmates on this unit with a variety of mental health diagnoses. This unit was kept cool throughout the year because the psychotropic medications the inmates were prescribed worked better within cool environments. The Sargeant ordered Dean to go on the unit with another officer, Officer Slick. He was a thin guy who looked like he spent a lot of time in front of the mirror admiring his own reflection. As he combed his hair back for the 20th time in front of Dean, he stated, "Here comes the nurse. I'll take Dean out there and show her what we do." The sergeant opened the officer station door first, then opened the two main interior corridor sliders to allow the nurse to enter another door, to pass medications. The door to the inmate pod was then opened to allow us all to enter. Upon seeing the nurse, the inmates quickly formed a line with their water cups to get their medication before breakfast arrived. Officer Slick opened the med room door so the nurse could enter. As Dean followed the nurse in, Officer Slick stayed outside the door to keep order. The inmates pushed each other, scrambling to run up in line while the other female officer left to get the breakfast cart. Breakfast was served after all inmates obtained their medications, then locked back in their perspective cells, and then later released into the dayroom when breakfast was served. Only 15 inmates were let out at a time due to the unit policy. After the first half were done getting medications, the next group was allowed out. Inmates were then let out to eat breakfast, 10 minutes of eating time, then locked in as the second half of the group was allowed out to eat as well. One male inmate apparently was homeless before arriving at the institution. Dean was told to watch him due to his theft of breakfast items. By the time breakfast was done, Officer Dean was scheduled to work in segregation. She could not get out of unit 3 fast enough due to such a welcoming crew.

Upon her arrival in segregation, there were four other male officers waiting to eye her up like a piece of meat. The door to the officer station was opened for her arrival. Sgt. Nims, along with three other male officers, instructed her to go out on the unit right away without introductions or radio. Officer Newton opened the door for her as they headed out to walk around the unit. Officer Newton stated, "Hey, wait here, I'll be right back!" Dean didn't know officer Newton ran through another walk-through door to the other side of the unit. Officer Dean was left alone on the floor as all the inmates were locked in their cells. She turned to look towards the officer's station and saw Officer Newton and the others laughing inside the officer's station. She knocked on the window of the officer station to have them let her in. Officer Newton slammed the trap closed, ignoring her as he continued to laugh. The unit soon became loud with screams in graphic detail of what the inmates would physically do to her. She became so scared she wanted to run to the door but resisted the urge after turning around in the direction of the officer station, seeing the laughter inside the bubble. She looked around at the many inmates yelling out of their cell doors. "Hey, bitch, would I like to fuck with you! Bring that pussy over here! Man, I can smell her over here!" when she spotted the instigator on the lower tier. Officer Dean slowly walked over to a very short man in cell 18. She stated, "Good morning, Sir." As the man on the other side of the thick metal cell door looked up at her through the spit-smeared filthy window, he stated, "You a tall glass of water, Miss! How tall are you?" Suddenly, it quieted down as the other inmates wanted to listen to their verbal exchange. She saw his name on the outside of the cell door and stated, "Good morning Mr. Malone, how would you feel if somebody talked that way to your mother, daughter, sister, or grandmother?" He responded, "I would not like that at all, Miss. In fact, I would kick their god-liven ass if they ever spoke to the members of my family that way! Who are you?" She responded by saying, "I'm Officer Dean, and I would in no way address you or anyone else here with such disrespect, ever." At this time, it became so silent, that you could hear a pin drop. Inmate Malone stated, "I can respect that!" Are you working our unit today?" She stated, "Not today, Mr. Malone; you have a good day, Sir!" She turned around and slowly walked over to the officer station as the unit appeared in disbelief or shock at what just transpired in front of them, co-workers and inmates. The silence, not only from the inmates but also from her co-workers, which resonated, suggesting their tactics of intimidation intended for new female staff was a senseless act contradicting what working as a team meant in this field. As Dean walked by the officer station window, she observed the mouths of her co-workers still hung open as she requested the sergeant to let her inside the officer station. Sgt. Nims opened the door as it became quiet inside that bubble. She sat down, asking to see the unit post orders as the two officers stopped giggling and then quickly vacated the bubble to conduct rounds. She looked at Sgt. Nims, nodded her head as he handed her the post-order booklet. He never gave her eye contact as if their little game did not work in running her off the unit. She was positive this was not the first time they did this to a new female officer. Word quickly got out about the way Officer Dean handled herself in Segregation. Her two hours in segregation went by quickly. It was time for Dean to go to her next assignment, unit 4.

Unit 4 was a unique unit. It was an open pod and open officer station. This floor was designated as a program floor for programing. This programing included addictions, domestic violence, anger issues, parenting classes, and school to obtain a GED. However, it was currently being used for addictions treatment. Each room had four beds, so it held more inmates. It also had a washer and dryer inmates could use for their clothing items when they were not participating in program activities. Unfortunately, several years later, she learned it only had a success rate of 1%, and she could understand why. Before Dean entered this unit, she saw several male officers hanging out in the pod. As Sgt.

Jacques opened the officer station door; he quickly introduced himself, then continued, as he crossed his arms and legs, "So why would a woman like yourself want to work in a dump like this?" Before she could answer, two more officers came over from the other side of the hall to introduce themselves to Dean. Officer Bills and Officer Schmoze, with their sweaty hands, shook her hand, stating, "Hello." Sgt. Jacques quickly distracted the attention given to the other officers by loudly stating, "You know they call me the chief around here, and I'm sleeping with my regular officer, who happens to be in my bed right now. So why are you here?" Dean stated quickly, "My priorities are my job, my children, and my education, and that's it!" Sgt. Jacques replied, "Good answer; because sex is my priority!" winking in my direction. The other male officers chuckled, then left quickly when Dean gave them a look. Dean wasn't on this unit very long before all the new officers were called to report to the administration office for orientation. As she was leaving, Sgt. Jacques said, "I hope to see more of you sometime!" as he giggled like a little schoolgirl as Officer Dean departed. Really.

As all of us met in the administration room, the captain asked us if we had any questions, problems, or concerns as they passed around the institution policies and procedures designated for the institution. Before we were to choose a shift or job, the captain answered the many questions our group had from their first day on the job. I also raised my hand. The captain called on me, "Yes, Officer Dean?" Dean went on to ask what their policy on sexual harassment was. The captain had this shocked look on her face. "Why, yes, we do. Can I ask why, Dean?" The reason why I'm asking is because one of your Sargeant's just stated his priority was sex and winked at me." The captain then asked which Sargent. I stated, "Sgt. Jacques, Madam." Apparently, he was called down to the captain's office prior to the end of his shift and talked to about his behavior. Years later, this same Sargent attended a Correctional Association Expo, exploring various vendors accompanied by several female staff members. It wasn't all he was exploring later that evening. He was allegedly caught doing sexually suggestive activities with several female attendees and was immediately fired. It was too bad they did not weed him out sooner.

Sadly, this would not be the first- or last-time events similar to this took place while Dean worked at the institution. Unbeknownst to Dean, it happened to be a regular occurrence for any female who worked at this facility, as well as other correctional facilities within the

24

state. Most of the time, it's something which goes unreported for the most part. Even when female officers do report such activities, it was never taken seriously. When female officers did report such inappropriate conduct, they were unexpectedly "blackballed or set up to be fired." Years had gone by when other male officers who worked in the office, reported they were instructed to shred incident reports, including reports of inappropriate conduct. This was just one incident out of thousands that Dean experienced, which never were reported out of fear of retaliation from fellow male officers and higher staff. Officer Dean could not tell you how many times male officers bragged about the size of their appendages, made sexual remarks, blocked her from moving out of an area, trapped her with their arms around her, grabbed or poked her, or denied a sexual incident took place by inmates seen by Dean, as she navigated her time throughout her career during her tenure with the Department of Corrections. Later, statistics showed that 20% of women who worked in corrections were the highest either fired, suspended or terminated for something, meanwhile male officers were part of the boy's club and no statistics have been reported.

I'll show you mine if you show me yours! No thanks

Chapter 3
Does the Institution sell Tootsie Rolls
on Canteen?

Based on her seniority, Dean was able to choose an available first-shift position. However, she soon learned that her rotation included working on the dreaded 9th floor, Unit 9C—the unit housing the most behaviorally challenging inmates—and under a sergeant known for being difficult to work with. During her first year, Officer Dean's rotation consisted of 9C, the 3rd floor, and escort duty.

During her time as a new correctional officer, being naive about odd behaviors was not a good thing; however, if you have never been exposed to these behaviors, how would you know? Officer Dean's rotation started with the 3rd floor after a two-week on-the-job training, otherwise known as OJT. This floor was considered the special needs unit. It was always cool year-round due to the medications prescribed, as spoken about in the first chapter, and because those who were prescribed such medications had a difficult time adjusting their internal body temperature. Officers loved this unit just because it was kept cool year-round. The other units did not have the luxury of having central air, so the officers and inmates sweat it out during the warmest months of the year. Before she even entered the officer station, Dean observed the female sergeant already sleeping on her desk, just like the first time she met this Sargent. As Dean entered the officer bubble with a happy greeting, "Good Morning, Sarg!" The Sgt was not as enthused so early in the morning, especially with the officer she tried to intimidate on the very first day.

This was Officer Slick's post. He worked this post every day and did not have a rotation to other jobs within the building. Today was the one day during the week, he got to work with officer Dean, otherwise, there was another officer who worked officer Slick's days off. The Sgt. got up from her chair slowly and finally introduced herself. As the Sargent placed her hands on her hips and shook her head from side to side, she stated, "You call me Sgt. Fudge! I didn't expect you to return after your first day! I expect you to do your fuckin job and don't fuck up my unit! When I tell you to do something, you fucken do it, hear me, Barbie Doll?" As the Sgt. spoke to me, she came closer and closer to my face where I could smell what she had for breakfast. Unless she ate shit, that's what I smelled. Dean, stated, "Yes, Madam!"

Now, to describe Sgt. Fudge was a relatively short, round woman who skipped wearing a bra, opting only for her uniform—which was extremely dirty, with the back of her collar blackened from God knows what. She always appeared exhausted and often slept at her desk during work hours. Dean really don't know why she was so tired or if she was coherent at times. If something happened, she would startle easily. Dean kept an open mind about this Sergeant, as we all know, we never know what is really happening after people go home, if they have a home, what they are dealing with outside of work, they may work another job or attend school. We don't know.

After Dean wiped the droplets of spit from her glasses, after the sergeant set the rules for her unit, Officer Slick giggled. The sergeant opened the officer station door to let Dean, along with Officer Slick, out on the floor to conduct morning count. The control sergeant made her morning announcement, "It is now time for the 0615-standing count!" Sgt. Fudge opened the 20 cell doors for the inmates to stand outside of. One by one, they quickly exited their cells to see Officer Dean, the brand-new officer with no strips. Officer Slick instructed Officer Dean to conduct her first count. Each inmate stood in front of their cell in twos. As Dean walked by each male inmate, they were smelling her without her noticing. She could hear the sniffing, as if everyone had allergies. She was so scared due to this being her official start by herself, she started to perspire. As she walked by one inmate, she had to do a double take. This man was standing in front of his cell with his cellmate, arms crossed, trying to hide his obvious breasts as he was transitioning. She continued to do her count, passing yet another unusual sight. This inmate had an enormous hand, wearing an ace bandage, tightly wrapped, causing it to cut his blood circulation off to his hand. His hand was extremely swollen as it appeared to be the size and appearance of something not of this world. She continued her count, passing an elderly man in a wheelchair who looked like he was wearing the same shirt for weeks. Covered in drool and snot, along with the smell, which was alarmingly pungent.

I counted 32 Sgt. Fudge!

Sgt. Fudge called in the count to control. The Lieutenant, who happened to be sitting inside control center, recorded it. Count was cleared 10 minutes later. All the inmates entered their cells to wash up for breakfast. Officer Slick went out to the elevator core to retrieve the breakfast cart. Together, they supervised the breakfast meal as the unit swamper handed out two milks, cereal, two slices of bread, and a fruit cup, one-by-one until everyone was seated. Officer Slick oversaw hiring the unit swamper. This was an inmate who helps the officer with cleaning, clothing exchanges, and anything the Sgt or officer asks him to do. The benefit of being the unit swamper was you got extra food, you were out of your cell most of the day, and you had your pick of the better clothing items.

One inmate, who was homeless prior to his incarceration, walked away with a loaf of bread stuck under his shirt, Officer Slick caught him before he returned to his cell. Officer Slick stated, "Dean, you gotta watch these guys! They will hide anything in their socks, pants, underwear, in their waistband, and under their shirt!" Officer Dean walked over to the inmate as he walked back to his cell and stated, "Sir, you will eat again in a few hours." He turned around and just looked at the new officer and replied, "Old habits are hard to break, Officer." He placed the loaf of bread in Dean's hand. As the meal was being cleaned up, the nurse arrived to hand out medications. Officer Slick told Dean to escort the nurse to the medication room and monitor meds while he took the tray cart back to the kitchen. Dean stated, "No problem, Slick!"

Officer Dean unlocked the medication room door and let the nurse in as the inmates ran back to their cells, grabbing their cups and water to stand in line, waiting their turn. The nurse stepped in and set –up her desk area for distribution. While Dean watched her get settled in, the inmates were already arguing about who was in line first, shoving each other, throwing cups, and just being disruptive. Officer Dean stated, "Guys, can I please get some order here? Line up please, single file!" Quickly listening to the officer's order, they lined up quickly. The inmate in the wheelchair came rolling out of his cell, extremely slow, towards the medical office. It was similar to watching someone who had stuff stuck to a shoe or hanging out of his pants, leaving a trail of debris behind him as dirty toilet paper was stuck to his seat. His odor proceeded him. Officer Dean stated, "Sir, we can get you some new clothes after we are done with meds, ok?" The inmate slowly looked up at the officer and stated, "No thanks. I like my clothes." The nurse quickly handed him his medications and sent him on his way. He turned his wheelchair around slowly and wheeled himself back towards his room as all the inmates in line covered their noses with their shirts to avoid smelling the stench. That was the moment Dean decided not to breathe through her nose but her mouth. The nurse whispered, "He refuses to take showers, and he has dementia." Officer Dean asked the nurse how long he had been on this unit. The nurse stated, "Oh, about a month, and I think he's showered once a week; he drools on himself, and the rotten food just builds up on his clothes." Meanwhile, someone threw something on the floor, and another inmate picked it up and threw it back toward another inmate. Officer Dean stated, "Ok, guys, enough please!" Dean asked about the inmate who had the swollen hand. The nurse responded, "He doesn't like his hand because he says it's evil so he's trying to get it amputated. He gets it infected by smearing fecal matter in open wounds on the hand. Believe me, it's well recorded."

The nurse was almost done when Officer Slick returned to the unit then proceeded to go back inside the officer station. As the nurse was leaving, something was being thrown around in the dayroom, again. Officer Dean decided to walk around the unit as the inmates were watching TV. One inmate was definitely wearing diapers under his state-issued prison uniform, as it appeared to be very bulky around his back side. He appeared to grab something from his back-pocket area, and then Dean noticed the inmate, who was in a wheelchair, observed placing his canteen-purchased sodas in his toilet. Officer Dean really did not know why he was doing that but continued to walk around the unit. Officer Slick decided to come back out on the unit and informed Officer Dean that we had to conduct clothing exchanges. As Dean looked inside the officer bubble, the sergeant appeared to be very tired, laying her head down on her desk. "Slick, is she always tired? Dean asked inquisitively. "Yeah, pretty much; she's always like that; I just do my job and go home." He responded. "So how does she know what's going on out on the floor?" she asked. Officer Slick responded, "I really don't care what she does. She's the sergeant. If shit goes down, she's responsible, so don't fuck anything up when she's here, ok?" Dean responded, "Ok."

So, while one-for-one exchanges were being conducted, an inmate ran out of his cell, complaining someone was throwing shit into his cell. Dean happened to see everyone sitting at the tables watching TV. Then Dean noticed the inmate wearing diapers was holding his hand behind his back. What are you doing, Sir? Dean asked. The inmate responded, "Nothing." As he chewed on whatever he had in his mouth. As all the inmates received their new clothing, Officer Slick took a set of clothes over to the inmate with the wheelchair. "It's shower day for you, so please go clean yourself up." The inmate swamper got the shower together for this inmate so he could wash up. It was a special shower with a rail to grab onto and a seat for those who had difficulty standing. He slowly made his way over to the shower as the inmates all clapped. It took this man well over a half hour to get to the shower before showering himself.

Dean sat out in the dayroom with the inmates as Officer Slick and Dean noticed an inmate pick up something off the floor and swallow it. "Slick! He just swallowed something he picked up from the floor!" Officer Slick responded, "Damn it! The nurse must have dropped a pen cap or something! That inmate has Pica. I forgot to tell you to make sure there is nothing on the floor, or he will find it and swallow it." Dean had no idea what it was, so she asked the inmate after Officer Slick went inside the officer station for a few minutes. "Sir, can I ask you a question, please?" He came over to Dean and sat down at the table. "Sure, you can, officer? Smiling. Officer Dean asked, "First, what is your name? I see you don't have your name tag on you." Inmates were required to wear their identification tags; otherwise, they could receive a ticket. He quickly patted himself down his front as if he was missing something, jumped up, and ran to his room to retrieve it, still placing it around his neck as he sat down across from her. "My name is Toby Jones, madam, I mean, Officer." excitedly. Officer Dean asked, "Mr. Jones, I just saw you pick up something off the floor and swallow it; "why?" Mr. Jones stated, "Well, officer, when I was a little boy, I was told by my mother I swallowed a penny when I was about three years old. My mother took me to the doctor, and he stated it would pass through into my stool. Well, my mother watched over me for two days until I passed that penny. It was the only time she spent with me because she worked a lot. After about a month, I missed her so much that I ate a blue crayon. She took me to the doctor, and the doctor stated it would pass, so she was told to watch for it. Therefore, within two days, it passed through and came out blue. I continued to swallow things as a habit to get attention." Well, now you have my attention, Mr. Jones." stated Officer Dean. "I saw you pick up something over there on the floor and swallow it, so what was it, and why do you continue to do this?" questioning Mr. Jones. He quickly lifted his uniform shirt and showed Officer Dean the protruding object from his abdomen and lower chest area. "Well, I swallowed this toothpaste tube, it unraveled inside my stomach, and now it's causing me so much pain, so I figured the doctor would do surgery on me to get it out if I make myself sick enough," stated Mr. Jones. Dean asked him how long he had been swallowing objects. "He responded, "Well, I'm 42 right now, hmm, since I was 3 years old." Mr. Jones stated, "I found a paperclip on the floor over there, so I swallowed it."

Officer Slick went into the officer bubble to write an incident report about Mr. Jones's behavior. Slick called Dean on her radio to return to the officer bubble. "Excuse me, Mr. Jones." As Dean got up from the table, she noticed the inmate with the diaper was watching her as he chewed on whatever he had in his mouth. She went back into the officer station. Officer Slick was writing an incident report of his observations of Mr. Jones. Sgt. Fudge lifted her head and stated, "Whenever you see behavior like that, write up an incident report so the nursing staff are aware. Got it, Barbie Doll!" Officer Slick asked Dean if she saw him swallow something. Officer Dean stated, "Mr. Jones saw a paperclip on the floor, so he swallowed it. Yes, he admitted to me he did it so the doctors would remove the toothpaste container protruding out of his chest. He lifted up his shirt and showed me his chest." stated Dean. Sgt. Fudge quickly asked Dean, "Did you fucken hear me, Barbie Doll! When I ask you a fucken question, answer me first?" Dean responded, "Yes, indeed, Sgt. Fudge, loud and clear, madam."

Officer Slick was getting ready to retrieve the lunch cart, so he told Officer Dean to secure all the cell doors as the inmates locked in. As soon as he made the announcement, He quickly left to retrieve the lunch cart.

Meanwhile, the inmate who wore a diaper came up to the officer station window to ask a question. Officer Dean asked him, "What do you need, Sir?" He was observed chewing on what appeared to be a tootsie roll-shaped object. He just stood there. Officer Dean then asked Sgt. Fudge if canteen sold tootsie rolls. Sgt. Fudge lifted her head off her desk with a start. "Oh, fuck! Davis is eating his shit again!" She immediately called the nurse. Officer Dean slowly turned back to look at inmate Davis. He was smiling as he bit off another piece of his turd. There were pieces sticking in his teeth as he smiled a big grin. Officer Slick returned and then sat down. He was unfazed at what he saw as he reached into his backpack, grabbed a chocolate candy bar, and then chewed on the candy bar. He looked at Officer Dean, laughing with chocolate in his teeth as she gagged. For the next two days after seeing that, Dean lost her appetite.

When officers see such grotesque behaviors or situations, over time, it often desensitizes a person who experiences these kinds of extreme acts, almost normalizing this behavior, while other officers experience PTSD, CPTSD, or are traumatized from observing those situations. This is something officers are not told about ahead of time. Even today, Dean still has flashbacks from some of the situations she came upon during her tour of duty, which still resonate.

Do you want a bite? Tasty…

Chapter 4
My name is not Muthafucker!

Officer Dean's rotation sent her to work on the tenth floor for three days out of her work week. It was the unit nobody wanted to work, with the Sargent nobody wanted to work with. The Sargent's name was Sgt. Looming, a very hard-nosed young woman who was about 20 years old. Sgt. Looming called everyone muthafucker. No names. Just muthafucker this, muthafucker that. Anytime she needed you to do something, she would say, "Muthafucker, go take the trash out of the unit!" Never giving a person eye contact; always with her back to you. Never face-to-face communication, even when she called you muthafucker.

My partner, Officer Smith, who worked on the unit next to me, hated working with her. He always complained about her attitude and how she addressed him, even though he was a 32-year-old man with small children at home. He would say, "I don't get it! She is so disrespectful to everyone! I hate working on this floor! I can't wait to transfer to another unit!"

This kind of treatment went on for the duration of Officer Dean's six-month probation period without a word said to Sgt. Looming. Although Dean only worked this unit three days in a row out of the seven days, it still wore on a person. Sgt. Looming did have strengths, as she was extremely organized, was very observant, and didn't take shit from anybody, not even Lieutenant Gerber.

Lieutenant Gerber frequently checked on the units to make sure everything was running smoothly. She would get feedback from the Sergeants about how the new officers were doing in each unit. Although she never really stayed long enough to watch the officers in action, her judgment relied on what the sergeants thought of the new officers. This is really not the best system for determining if an officer is going to work out or not. People have their favorites, and not everyone is going to like you. If the sergeant does not like you or sees you as a threat, your long-term employment could be jeopardized just because you may not fit into the established clique.

As in every workplace, there are always going to be cliques, people who hang out together at work and after work. They go out, drink together most of the time and end up spending more time with each other than with their own families. Officers work the holidays, days off, multiple shifts, and get called in when emergencies occur. This is the life of the correctional officer. Because there are many people who are friends, it is very difficult to be accepted in the beginning; however, some people will come around, while some refuse to greet you or have a conversation. This has become a common problem with new officers. Because Dean worked just as hard as the other officers did, she hoped she could earn the respect of the staff just as the offenders had of her.

Sgt. Looming was not the kind of person to be warm and fuzzy to any officer. In fact, she was the one sergeant no one wanted to work with, which made it extremely difficult to fill the other officer post on her unit. It was a week before Officer Dean's six-month probation would be up, and she found herself assigned to work in the front lobby with Sgt. Monroe.

Sgt. Monroe was a no-nonsense kind of person, but he happened to be extremely respectful to all people he encountered. Because it was a central institution, it did not have a whole lot of diversity within its ranks. There were only a few correctional staff members who happened to be Caucasian working at this institution. Normally, Caucasian people transfer out as soon as they pass their probationary period to other prisons north of the institution unless they live within central city. Officer Dean was determined to stay at this institution for now until she finished school. This will be another chapter.

Sgt. Monroe was very nice and greeted all the visitors respectfully coming into the reception area. The families wanted to speak to their loved or liked ones on video screens. This institution had no contact visiting, which means their loved or liked ones could only see them through a computer screen, which was timed automatically to shut off after a given period. Two women came in to see their brother, who happened to be incarcerated at the institution at the time, so they came up to the counter ahead of others standing in line. Sgt. Monroe told the women to go to the other officer, who was Officer Dean because there was no line for her. They refused and stated, "We don't want to talk to that white bitch! We want you to take care of us!" Sgt. Monroe then stated quickly, "Well, that means you two will be leaving then because you just disrespected that officer, so leave!" These two women were so surprised by the sergeant's response that they started cussing him out. "Who do you think you are, muthafucker? You don't tell me where I need to go!" Sgt. Monroe stated, "If you don't leave, I'll call the police! They are right down the street. Now leave!" Both the women backed away from the visitor's check-in counter and then went to the bathroom before leaving. When they left, they ran out of the building. Since the bathroom was right in front of the visitors' front desk, it was easy to watch the comings and goings from that bathroom. Officer Dean was still in shock at what transpired. She had to use the bathroom after the last two visitors were taken care of. She observed no one enter the ladies' restroom after those two ladies were told to vacate the property by Sgt. Monroe. Dean informed Sgt. Monroe had to use the lobby bathroom, then got up and walked across the visitors' center to the women's bathroom. As she opened the door, she saw the walls covered entirely in what appeared to be blood. Someone used their tampon, which were left in the sink; and wiped menstrual blood all over the walls, the floors, the toilet, the mirror, and the sink. Officer Dean was stunned and shocked by this sight as it was one of the grossest things, to date, she had ever seen a woman do in retaliation. Dean reported the incident to Sergeant Monroe, and in turn, he immediately made a phone call to the supervisor's office. The supervisor had several swampers come down with buckets of bleach to clean up the mess left behind by the women. One of the women who came in inadvertently left behind their identification card due to being so angry at Sargent Monroe for referring them to Officer Dean for help. Since he had the woman's identification card, he handed it to the supervisor, along with an incident report of what the woman did in the lobby bathroom. Apparently, the supervisor later sent out a letter, including the identification card, placing a permanent ban on the woman to never be allowed back on the property. Officer Dean was grateful to Sergeant Monroe for sticking up for her. He later gave her a fist bump and stated, "We officers stick up for our own." This incident was the first indication to Officer Dean that she was accepted.

Officer Dean finally completed her probationary period at the institution and had to work with Sgt. Looming the very next day. As always, the Sgt. called her officers "Muthafuckers" for half the day until it was time for the officers to eat after the inmate lunch meal was completed. Officer Dean turned around in her chair to finally get some resolution or start an argument, either way, but it was going down today. Therefore, Officer Dean decided to not back down and talk to the Sargent about her selective word usage. Dean stated, "Sgt? Do I do everything you ask of me?" The sergeant had her back to Officer Dean, stating, "Yeah." Officer Dean continued, "I just wanted to tell you how well organized you are and that you run a good unit. However, I just wanted to ask you why you continue to call me a muthafucker instead of my name?" Sgt. Looming quickly turned her chair around and faced Officer Dean for the first time in six months. She stated, "That's the way my mutha and I talk to each other." Dean informed Sgt. that she would never talk to her own children that way, let alone staff. Sgt. Looming quickly responded by asking, "You got kids?" Dean replied, "Yes, and two are older than you." Sgt. Looming acted as if she was in shock. She got up out of her chair and sat in the corridor for about 45 minutes. Officer Dean didn't know what was going on and why she was sitting on the floor in the corridor. After 45 minutes, she came back into the officer station, never apologizing. However, she started addressing Officer Dean as Dean and not muthafucker anymore. Anytime Sgt. Looming had a problem with an officer on her unit, she would always ask to see if Officer Dean was working that day. Sgt. Looming would ask Lieutenant Gerber if she could send up Officer Dean to replace the officer she was working with. They became friends after that.

Sgt. Looming continued to call the other officers, "MuthaFuckers!"

We expect to be called all kinds of things by the inmates but not the staff. It was about common courtesy and respect for one another. At the end of the day, we depended on each other so we could go home to our loved and liked ones.

Chapter 5
Sometimes, you need to see it to believe it.

Officer Dean continued to do her job, day in and day out. She made sure those who she oversaw would be taken care of in regard to meals, clothing, and medical care, even though they were inmates. She saw them as human beings first. She never thought of using epithets towards inmates or staff. Always treating everyone with respect and dignity is what she was taught at the academy and a valuable lesson she learned in life. Period.

There were times Dean saw staff or inmates do things that were mind-boggling and unbelievable. Take, for instance, a situation in which staff was given an order by the sergeant to clean out a cell after a person was either sent to segregation or transferred out of the institution. She would place their property into their bin to be inventoried by the property sergeant.

Dean was working her rotation and had to work the third floor with Sgt. Fudge one day. This day happened to be a day in which the well-known elderly man, who smelled putrid, was leaving the institution to be transferred to another institution for his crime. He was the wheelchair-bound, elderly man who never liked to shower. He was one of the dirtiest, unkempt men on the unit, as first discussed previously. He drooled and had problems by frequently urinating on himself but chose not to bathe as often as he should have. Yes, he chose not to shower after he had an accident. I believe he had dementia, among a few other mental health issues.

Captain Mac, a former Marine, came on the unit to inform Sgt. Fudge to pack up the elderly man with all of his belongings to be moved out, then proceeded to have the two escort officers with him assist in getting this man ready for transport out of the institution. It took at least a half hour just to get the elderly man out of his bunk and seated into his wheelchair. The man wanted to pack his own items; however, Officer Dean was present and was given an order to get a bag to place all the elderly man's property inside of it. Captain Mac was assisting the escort officers and saw what was inside the cell. Officer Dean went back into the officer station to get a bag, as the captain requested. Sgt. Fudge ordered Officer Dean to stay inside the officer station because she wanted to take care of packing his property. The Sergeant quickly grabbed a bag and then proceeded to leave the officer's station to talk to Captain Mac out on the floor and assure him the property would be packed and then brought to his office within the next hour. Officer Dean opened the doors to let Captain Mac, the escort officers, along with the elderly inmate, off the unit as Captain Mac waved to Dean.

Captain Mac was well respected at the institution. He worked hard and recognized those officers who also held that same work ethic. He quickly recognized Officer Dean's work, her positive attitude, and her support of other officers, which led to her quick response to situations that could have escalated quickly without her intervention. The respect he held for Dean was recognized by higher-ups after several incidents and her documentation of events. If he needed assistance, he knew he could depend on her for support.

Officer Dean proceeded to watch Sgt. Fudge go into the elderly man's cell to pack up his property. Dean watched the Sergeant looking around for a bit before eyeing something left in this man's dirty toilet. Apparently, this man kept his soda cold by placing it in his toilet, as Dean had observed in the past. Officer Dean was aghast to watch the sergeant grab one bottle of soda out of the toilet, unscrew the cap, and proceed to drink this man's soda. Dean was close enough to the officer stations inside window to observe the water from this man's toilet slowly running down the bottle towards the sergeant's mouth. The drips of water from the bottle had stained the front of her blue shirt. Then she looked through this man's canteen purchases and found about 10-12 bags of chips, then proceeded to tear one bag open. She then proceeded to sit on his bunk, where he peed while eating a bag of chips as she was going through his property. Mind you, this elderly inmate drooled, had rotten food hanging on his shirt, and always smelled like urine as long as Officer Dean worked this unit over the last 8 months. The stench resignating from that room must have been atrocious.

Sgt. Fudge came back to the officer station and shoved a small bag into Officer Dean's chest, stating, "Take that bag down to the captain's office; he's waiting for it!" The Sgt. opened the door to let Dean out of the unit, and she headed directly to Captain Mac's office as ordered. Captain Mac was reading some paperwork when Officer Dean arrived. "What's this?" asked Captain Mac. Officer Dean responded by stating that Sergeant Fudge had told her to bring this bag to you and had set it down on his desk. The captain stood up, moving out of his chair to look at the small bag sitting on his desk. He placed gloves on before opening the bag. "Dean, this is not all of that inmate's property; there was a lot more! Hell, this guy just ordered quite a bit of canteen. Where is the rest?" Officer Dean stated, "Sgt.

Fudge cleaned out the cell, Sir, and this is what she gave me to give you, Captain." The captain opened the bag to see one bottle of soda and two bags of chips. "Where's the rest of it, Dean? Dean responded, "Sorry, Captain, I was just told to bring this bag to you. That's all I know." The captain looked at Dean and said, "Sgt. Fudge gave this to you? Dean responded, "Yes, Sir." Captain Mac stated, "What the hell, Dean! You saw what that inmate had in his cell, didn't you?" Yes, I did, Captain, yes, I did."

I'm watching MY show!

Now, every unit has TV sets hanging from the ceiling, so everyone has an opportunity to watch something on television during the day. Not everyone wants to watch what is playing on TV, so there will be disagreements or fights about what to watch. However, Officer Dean never expected what was about to go down on Unit 3. The Sergeant scheduled to work with Officer Dean was a petite woman with long blond braids named Sgt. Boch. She was about 4 ft. tall and 80 lbs. wet. What a character. She was on the phone talking to her clique of female friends stating, "Got stuck down here with this white bitch. What's her name?"

At this point, I am already feeling the love.

It was time for the 0615-standing count, and Sgt. Boch finally let Dean out on the unit to conduct the morning counts with Officer Slick. However, Officer Slick had other ideas. He decided he was going to stay in the officer station to tickle and screw around with Sgt. Boch. After the count was called, Sgt. Boch opened the doors to let the inmates out so Dean could start count. While Dean was counting, all the inmates heard was loud giggling coming from the officer station. Dean called in the count to Sgt. Boch, "25 Sergeant!" Sgt. Boch did not hear Dean over the radio, nor did she hear the nurse buzzing the door to get in to pass medications prior to breakfast. The Sergeant and Officer Slick were laughing and tickling each other, then Sgt. Boch appeared to fall off her chair. Meanwhile, control was trying to call to get the count for the unit so they could clear count. Then Dean hears over the loudspeaker, "Sgt. Boch, Please call Control Center immediately!" Apparently, the Captain was waiting patiently as well. Finally, I saw Sgt. Boch get off the floor and grab the phone to call in count. She then yells at Officer Dean, "How many, Dean? 25!" Then, count cleared so the sergeant could open the door for the nurse to conduct a medication pass. As Dean watched over the nurse distributing the medication, the inmate who had Pica (the eating of random non-edible objects) came to the officer station window to talk to Sgt. Boch. He happened to be upset because somebody threw a turd into his cell. Sgt. Boch stated, "Seriously! Are you gonna come to my window and complain about a turd? Are you sure it's a turd?" The inmate stated, "You can come see for yourself, Sgt." At that point, Sgt. Boch decided she was going to come out of the officer station to check out his turd story and then watch her Sunday religious show on TV since it was Sunday, of course. The captain had come and gone after checking out what was transpiring on the unit. So, Sgt. Boch leaves Officer Slick inside the officer's station so she could go look inside the inmate's cell. She sees what appears to be a turd on his cell floor, just as he stated there was. She had the inmate pick it up with toilet paper and throw it in his toilet.

Sgt. Boch proceeds to sit at one of the tables then turns the channel to her religious program. As she sat there, another inmate walked behind her to the inmate's cell, who just complained about the turd, and threw another one in his cell. The Sgt. just sat there listening to the singing of love and rejoicing when he started yelling to get her attention. Officer Dean was still with the nurse as she finished distributing medications to the last few stragglers who were stumbling in to get their medication. Sgt. Boch yelled back at the inmate who told her about the turd, "What the fuck is wrong with you! Can't you see I'm watching my religious program, Muthafucker!"

The inmate got so upset at her that he ran to his room and locked his cell closed. He then was trying to find something to swallow, such as his toothpaste tube and what appeared to be a pen cap, which he found on the dayroom floor. Sgt. Boch stated, "Everyone lock in now!" The nurse just finished with medications and was let out of the pod by Officer Slick. Sgt. Boch yelled over the radio, "We have a non-compliant inmate on unit 3!" Officer Dean had to help get everyone locked in quickly before the team arrived to escort the inmate off the unit. Captain Mac, who came down earlier to check the unit after Sgt. Boch delayed the count and arrived with a team to take the inmate to segregation. Captain Mac asked Sgt. Boch, what did the inmate do? She went on to state, "He got upset, ran to his room, and locked himself in." The captain asked why was he upset? Sgt. Boch stated, "Someone threw shit in his room, so he locked himself in his room." Captain Mac asked Dean if that was what happened. Since Dean could not confirm because she was with the nurse, she stated, "He did report somebody threw a turd in his room earlier, Captain." The captain just looked hard at Sgt. Boch as she continued to not pay attention to him while she watched her religious program.

He then decided to get the inmate out and have him escorted to segregation. As Captain Mac left the unit, he waved at Dean.

So much for religious programing…

Chapter 6
A Hard Pill to Swallow

Every day, Officer Dean had to assist the nurse with medication pass no matter what floor she worked. The Officer stood by so no fights would break out in line while the inmates waited for their turn to get their medications. Today was no different than any other day as the inmates jockeyed for a position in line while the nurse prepared herself. Her job was very stressful. She had to read each order and then pop their pills into a cup for them. Some inmates had multiple medications to take which took longer to pop out, while all the inmates were getting antsy, standing in line.

Officer Dean noticed an inmate cheeked his medication, not swallowing it. She called him out on it and had him open his mouth to verify if he still had it in his mouth. Mr. Pitts refused to open his mouth and acted as if he was insulted by the insinuation. He sat down in the dayroom, arms crossed, acting as if he was having a temper tantrum. Meanwhile, two inmates started a fight in the dayroom. Dean had to act fast, deciding to lock the nurse in the medication room for her safety with the cart of medications, while she informed the fill-in Sargent, there was a fight and to call for back-up. She informed everyone to lock in! Dean ran to secure all the cell doors while the fight continued. One inmate was getting kicked in the head and stomach area, and the other inmate was obviously the aggressor. She yelled at the aggressor to stop several times to no avail. He continued to assault the young inmate, who was curled up in a ball on the floor, as he protected his face from the onslaught of punches and kicks. Officer Dean decided to grab the assailant and proceeded to pin him up against the wall. She then cuffed his ass so quickly; he didn't know what happened. She asked the young inmate if he was ok. He stated, "Yes, I'll be ok. He was trying to have me give him my medications, and when I said no, he started to beat me up." Dean stated she would have a nurse look at him because he had received a bloody nose during the ruckus. Finally, the team arrived to assist. Sgt. Hopper, from across the hall, had to wait for an officer to come into the bubble before he could leave to run to the other side. Since Dean worked on the 10th floor, it took approximately 8-10 minutes for the team to arrive to help. Between the slow elevators and the control center having to open multiple doors, it was amazing an officer could get control over the situation so quickly, as did Officer Dean.

Captain Mac finally arrived with the team and stated, "Great job, Dean!" He then escorted both inmates to segregation as a policy when there was a fight. Captain Mac yelled, "Dean, have that report on my desk before the end of your shift!" He then left with both inmates, along with several other officers, escorting both gentlemen off the unit. Sgt. Hopper came up to Officer Dean and stated, "Damn good job, girl!" and high-fived her! He then went back to his unit across the hall.

Many years later, Dean was working at another maximum-security institution up north. She happened to be working a program unit for inmates who were just released from segregation or restrictive Housing Unit (RHU) on third shift that day. She recognized the same inmate who claimed he didn't cheek his medication that day at the institution many years ago. Dean was conducting routine rounds when the inmate recognized her, asking, "Didn't you work at the institution many years ago, officer? Her response was, "Yes, I did. I recognize you, Mr. Pitts, you were the one who claimed you swallowed your medication, but I saw you cheek it. Then you sat down in the dayroom having a temper tantrum." Mr. Pitts stated, "You remember that? You have a good memory, Officer." He laughed a little, then responded, "Yeah, I'll be honest, I did cheek my medication that day and was mad you caught me. It was for my schizophrenia because it made me feel funny. Now I'm on a different medication. I won't be doing that again around you. Nice to see you, Officer!" Dean stated, "I can't say the same to you, Mr. Pitts, because you are back in here, again. You take care of yourself and take your medication, okay?" Mr. Pitts stated, "Ok, officer, thanks for talking." He then went back to his bunk to sleep.

You call people out on their shenanigans, and they will remember you, hopefully in a positive light like this exchange. Some memories are imprinted from the past which a person never seems to forget. Dean wished he would have told her then what was going on, and maybe she could have alerted the psychiatrist so he would not have had to wait so long to be prescribed the right medication that worked for him.

You never know whose life you will save, again!

Officer Dean worked several different units at the institution along with escorting once a week. Today, Dean had to work with Sgt. Peckel on unit nine for the week due to shortness of staff. Peckel was a racist and misogynist, who got great pleasure in calling inmates epithets, as well as played games to piss people off. He was one of those guys who worked out a lot but had no common sense. Female officers hated working with him due to his inappropriate comments to fellow staff and inmates alike. So today was NOT Officer Dean's lucky day. She planned on staying out on the floor the entire day with the inmates.

Unit nine received a new inmate named Mr. Jordan, who was escorted to the ninth floor by two staff. Mr. Jordan came in and had a bullet lodged in his leg, limping slowly on the unit. Dean had him go to a lower bunk due to his injury, even though he was assigned an upper bunk. Sgt. Peckel informed Dean, "He can fucken climb on the top bunk, that mother fucker!" Dean explained the inmate could not climb on top due to his injury. Peckel stated, "I don't give a Fuck, Dean! He can go lie down on the floor, then! Fucken nappy headed mutherfucker!" Officer Dean called Captain Mac about the bunk change due to Sgt. Peckel not wanting to do his job. Captain Mac approved the change. The inmate on the lower bunk was asked to change bunks; seeing the terrible shape Mr. Jordan was in, he was happy to switch.

Mr. Jordan had to go out for surgery in a few days due to his injury. When Dean asked him what happened, Mr. Jordan was honest, stating, "I was trying to get money from someone who owed me, then my gun accidentally went off, hitting me in my leg." "Damn, Mr. Jordan!" said Dean. Mr.

Jordan went on to say, "You know, if you are on paper and the cops get involved, it's an automatic probation violation because I'm not supposed to have a gun on me. But I was scared." Just then, Captain Mac must have called Sgt. Peckel on his shit and informed him to place the inmate on the lower bunk. Sgt. Peckel was not happy; but livid. Mr. Jordan was informed to go to the lower bunk by Sgt. Peckel over the loudspeaker, so he limped to his cell to unpack his property.

A few days later, Officer Dean had to again work with Sgt. Peckel. There was another inmate who was complaining about his leg hurting really bad. This inmate saw Officer Dean and stated, "I've been placing warm compresses on my wound, and it seems to be getting worse." Dean asked Sgt. Peckel if he could call a nurse to look at the inmate's leg. Sgt. Peckel stated, "Fuck no, he can submit paperwork if he wants to be seen, same as the rest of these mother fuckers!" Sgt. Peckel left the unit to go wander around somewhere; that's when Officer Dean made the move to call a nurse to the unit. She was able to get a nurse to see the inmate quickly, defying Sargent's request to submit a blue doctor slip. Unfortunately, Sgt. Peckel arrived at the same time as the nurse and then proceeded to ask her why she was there. Dean heard the nurse state, "I was called up here, so now I'm following up with the officer." Sgt. Peckel became so angry that he called the captain to have Officer Dean written up for insubordination due to her defying his order. The nurse was allowed to enter the unit to see the inmate in question. Dean called Mr. Jones over to the nurse's office to check his leg. As Officer Dean stood outside the nurse's office, she could see Sgt. Peckel screaming into the phone, arguing with the Captain and Dean could see his face turn red from anger. The nurse had Mr. Jones sit outside the nurse's office as she was contacting someone.

Apparently, the nurse contacted control center for an ambulance, due to Sgt. Peckel, utilizing the phone, still yelling. The unit manager came over to inform Officer Dean to have everyone locked in except Mr. Jones. While she had everyone lock in, Captain Mac showed up on the unit with the ambulance crew to take Mr. Jones to the hospital. The nurse came out of her office and stated, "Mr. Jones is going to the hospital; ASAP! Please get your unit workers to wipe everything down on your unit!" Officer Dean asked the nurse what the problem was and why we had to wipe everything down. The nurse pulled Dean off to the side and stated, "Mr. Jones has the MRSA virus, and it's highly contagious. Since he has diabetes also, it spreads faster due to his compromised health. So, wipe everything down and wear gloves if you handle his property." Dean had never heard of MRSA before or that it was seriously contagious.

As the ambulance crew was leaving, Captain Mac escorted them back down to intake, as he left, he waved and stated, "Great job, Dean!" Sgt. Peckel was livid. Dean supplied the unit swampers with gloves and helped them wipe everything on the unit down with a strong mixture of solutions designed to kill the MRSA virus. Dean really didn't know about this virus or what it does to a person. A few inmates yelled, "Dean, why are you helping wipe down the unit?" Dean replied, "If you guys get sick, most likely I will contract it too!" The entire unit was wiped down, from the traps to countertops, and where everyone on the unit got water and ice. Fortunately, only one other inmate contracted the virus, and it was Mr. Jones's cellmate. Mr. Greek was escorted off the unit the next day for a sick call. As Dean was escorting the next day, she brought Mr. Greek down to be seen. She had the doctor take a look at Mr. Greek's elbow. The doctor numbed the area on Mr. Greek's elbow and proceeded to make a cut to drain the puss as Dean had to look away. Mr. Greek said, "It's ok Officer, I don't feel a thing. You don't like seeing that do you?" Dean stated,

"Nope, I could never be a nurse, Mr. Greek. I just couldn't."
Mr. Greek stated, "I'll be ok, officer. I'll be ok."

While Dean worked at the institution, she happened to meet and marry her long-time sweetheart, Officer J. Purtue, who was the best person ever to enter Dean's life. They were married nine years later after meeting at the prison. They never worked together, but a loving impression continued to last long after she walked out of her job at the institution after almost four years of service. More will be written in volume 2. So if officer Dean's name changes to Officer Purtue in the story, it's then she was already married and starting working at another institution.

Years later, while working at another maximum-security prison, Mr. Jordan, who accidently shot himself in the leg years prior, was escorted to Officer Purtue's unit, Unit 22. Purtue took this big end unit of 100 inmates because it rhymed with Purtue. Every time Purtue answered the unit phone, she would say, "Unit 22, Purtue!" The receiver always chuckled, which was done on purpose to get people to laugh.

The escorting officer dropped Mr. Jordan's bag of clothes on the dayroom table as Mr. Jordan slowly walked, utilizing a walker. Purtue noticed he was dragging his right leg, and the right leg was three times the size of his left leg. He happened to recognize Officer Purtue right away. "I remember you! You worked at the institution some years back, but your name was Dean, as I recall!" You know you saved my life!" stated Mr. Jordan. Purtue started to recognize Mr. Jordan from all those years ago. She started smiling, stating, "Mr. Jordan! What is going on with you!" He went on to state, "Well, I got shot, and the bullet is in my hip. Some guy was trying to rob me in my wheelchair after I cashed my SSI check." Purtue had a suspicion something was definitely wrong with his right leg because one was so swollen. Mr. Jordan's right foot appeared twisted as he dragged it on the floor as he walked with the walker. Officer Purtue asked Mr. Jordan to have a seat in the day room and proceeded to call Health Services Unit (HSU).

The nurse in the Health Services Unit answered the call. Officer Purtue described what was going on with the inmate in question. The nurse replied, "Well, maybe he has a fat leg and a thin leg!" Purtue persisted in advocating on behalf of the inmate, "I suspect something is not right due to him being shot on that side. Can you please see him? It could be blood clots or something! Can I get your name so I can write it in my logbook to document you are refusing to see him?" So, finally, the nurse stated, "Fine, send him up then, and we'll take a look." Officer Purtue had an inmate swamper get a wheelchair to escort Mr. Jordan to HSU to be seen, then placed his belongings in a bag, just in case he went out to the hospital. About 20 minutes later, the nurse contacted Officer Purtue, indicating Mr. Jordan was being sent out to the hospital. Officer Purtue was aghast by the intake nurse sending him to a unit in the condition he was in and never noticed his leg, just gave him a walker instead. This man could have died on her unit. Talk about apathy for another human being.

Approximately two months later, Mr. Jordan was escorted back to another unit close to Officer Purtue. He was being wheeled towards Officer Purtue as she was standing in the middle of the hallway watching approximately 100 inmates returning from recreation when suddenly, Mr. Jordan started yelling down the hallway, "See that woman, she saved my life! Not once, but twice! Listen to her guys and do right, all respect Officer Purtue!" He was so excited to tell Purtue thank you that he started crying, wanting so badly to fist bump her for helping him, yet again! He rolled up by Officer Purtue in front of several male officers and stated, "You have no idea what you did for me, Ms. I had seven blood clots in my leg! I could have died! You saved my life, and I truly thank you!" Mr. Jordan started wiping the tears away with his right hand. Officer Purtue stated, "You are welcome, Mr. Jordan! There was a reason why we met again; now, do right for yourself, ok?" He was so thankful; he continued to wipe tears away as he was rolled back to the unit next to where Officer Purtue worked.

The male officers standing next to her were not as thrilled.

While at another institution, Officer Purtue happened to be finishing her classes at a local university to complete her bachelor's degree in psychology when she needed a class in biology

From: Radjack, Barry M - DOC
Sent: Monday, August 10, 2015 9:57 PM
To: Arndt, Davis R - DOC; Purtue, Lisa A - DOC
Subject: Good Job

Lt. Arndt,

On Friday August 7, 2015 I received a call from CO Purtue on unit # 23 stating that she believes that an inmate needed to be seen by Prime Care HSU to assess a problem with his leg. She stated that she has observed the inmate over time and is concerned by the change in his condition. In fact she was 100% correct and possibly may have prevented a serious condition from occurring by calling the HSU and insisting that we see the PT. I assessed the PI. and referred him to WMH- ER for further care and treatment which was definitely needed at that time. Just wanted to let you know that we get many calls in the HSU for assistance from various units in the facility and they get overwhelming at times, but the diligence of CO Purtue on this occasion was greatly appreciated by all HSU staff and especially the PI.

Kudos to CO Purtue☺

to finish her semester's work. This wonderful professor assigned all the students to write a paper on a genetic disease. Purtue was dead set on learning more about the populations she supervised, so she chose the disease, Sickle Cell. A genetic blood disease that makes the red blood cells appear like half-moon shapes (otherwise known as sickle-shaped cells) which cause great discomfort to the carrier. The sickle-shaped cells feel as though the carrier has pins and needles throughout their body, on the inside. When a carrier is in crisis, they are not receiving enough oxygen to their lungs, and the pain is everywhere. It can also shut down organs if not addressed quickly.

There happened to be a new inmate placed on Purtue's unit who did not share with the nurse practitioner he had Sickle Cell Anemia upon entry into the institution. He was only on this unit for approximately a day or so until he started experiencing symptoms of his disease. As Purtue was conducting her rounds, he told her he was not feeling well and just wanted to see a doctor, with no explanation. She quickly grabbed a blue slip so he could fill it out. He then placed it under his door to get picked up later when she conducted rounds again. She later checked on him as he was seated up against his cell door, exhibiting pain all over his body. Purtue asked him if he was ok. He stated, "Officer, I have sickle cell, and I'm having a hard time breathing right now. I didn't tell the health staff here because I thought I would not be here long. I'm having a hard time… breathing." Officer Purtue immediately contacted the Health Services Unit to report what his name was and what he was experiencing at the time. Health Services On call male nurse later contacted Purtue to inform her he had no record of him having sickle cell. Purtue stated, "He stated he didn't tell the nursing staff upon entry because he didn't think he would be here very long. Can I please get someone down here to look at him, please?" The male nurse was getting more agitated by the moment, refusing because it was not in his health records, so the nurse thought the inmate was messing with staff. The nursing staff contacted the captain to come down to Purtue' s unit to see what the problem was. The captain arrived with two extra officers to see what was going on with this inmate. The inmate told the captain he was having a hard time breathing due to his condition. The captain finally contacted the nurse to have them come down to the unit to examine the inmate's condition. The male nurse was extremely angry as he arrived since he had to walk down the hallway to see this guy. The nurse was red-faced, mad he had to assess this inmate's condition. Purtue watched this nurse as he slammed himself on a chair to speak to this inmate in a side room to see what was going on due to thinking the inmate was making up stories.

This nurse was completely red in the face until he realized the inmate was telling the truth. The nurse's red face from anger soon dissipated as the inmate was exhibiting clear symptoms of being in a sickle cell crisis. The nurse had to get some medication for the evening to comfort him before making any calls. As Purtue learned later, the following morning, the inmate was taken to the hospital for a blood transfusion and had to stay at the hospital for two nights following this event. It pays to be diligent when it comes to someone's life in your hands.

When Purtue returned to class, she shared her story with the biology professor. She was so excited that Purtue took the initiative to learn more about this genetic disease to recognize when someone was in crisis. It actually saved a man's life. They hugged each other as Purtue thanked the professor for taking the time to teach the class these very critical aspects of human biology.

There are reasons why we meet people along our journey. Sometimes God may send someone back to us because he knows our heart is pure and we will do the right thing on their behalf. It's extremely fulfilling to see people remember you for the good you've done for them.

There is a very famous poet by the name of Dr. Maya Angelou who stated, "I've learned that people will forget what you said, people will forget what you did, but people will never forget how you made them feel." (insert Email).

This incident got the attention of superiors, who decided to call Purtue to the supervisor's office. Anytime an officer gets called to the supervisor's office, it wasn't good.

Officer Purtue was called down to the captain's office by a second shift captain whose name was Capt. Napoleon. Capt. Napolean was a short stature of a man who bragged about all the toys he bought with all the overtime he works. Officer Purtue would overhear all his conversations with the third shift officer on Unit 2 at the other maximum prison she worked at. When he was held over for third shift, he would hang out on this unit for hours drinking coffee. The smell of butterscotch coffee would permeate the hallways leading to unit 2. The unit 2 Sargent would tell Purtue, "He sits here drinking all my coffee because he's over tired. He brags about when he's going to retire in a few years. He's such an ass." Purtue would chuckle after the Sargent would hand her a cup of coffee then return to the upstairs unit to finish her stats assignments for college while doing periodic rounds.

Anyway, Purtue arrived at the captain's office for what she thought she did wrong, again. This time the captain asked her what she was as he yelled at her stating, "Who are you? An EMT, a nurse, what!" Purtue stated, "I'm a mom. I've seen things in my life and I'm just following the DOC code which states… She went on to clearly recite the DOC code and what it said. Purtue stated, "If you see something, say something. It states this in the DOC code." All officers needed to know the DOC codes by heart as we wrote incident reports that could go to court. Captain Napoleon stated, "Well, I'm giving you an order to stop calling HSU for these guys, they are Fucken Felons! As he started yelling at Purtue, sticking his finger in her face as his face started turning red. Purtue stated, "So you are telling me to defy the DOC code, 303…" and she went on to state the code per the rule book. She then stated, "I will continue to call HSU because these inmates are human beings. Everyone who I contacted HSU for was sent out to the hospital. If they need emergency medical care, I will continue to call per the DOC code." Captain Napoleon turned red in the face because he knew she was right. Purtue stated, "Is that all?" He gave her a 6-month review of average and sent her on her way. This entire incident happened in front of a female Lieutenant.

Purtue became a target. More will be written in another volume of what happened to Officer Purtue.

Chapter 7
We got a Cutter!

People who come into the correctional system are booked in, stripped out, asked to squat- cough- and lift their genitals and/or breasts. Then they are supplied with a small sliver of soap and lice shampoo to prevent outbreaks of infestation then expected to shower. During this time, the officers working within intake can spot gang tattoos, cutters or slicers and dicers, drug users by their tracks, and homeless, quickly. The revealing scars on the inner arms, wrists, thighs, anywhere your imagination can take you can blatantly be seen. Cutting is a mental health condition resulting in the release of pain or stress for the cutter. Great care and supervision are given to these individuals, if officers are made aware of by nursing staff to take heed. Sometimes officer's working the units, are not told or don't pay attention.

Officer Dean was working as an escort with her partner Officer Johnston. Officer Johnston was the oldest officer in Dean's academy class who could outrun, outshoot or out do any of their classmates' half his age. He was a great officer. Dean really looked up to him and felt as though she would always be protected by him, which he had several times.

Both Dean and Johnston received an emergency call from the Control Center to report to Unit 3, the Special Needs Unit. When there was an emergency, a Lieutenant or Captain must respond to the unit before the line staff could do anything regarding an inmate. Today, that inmate was slicing himself to shreds. As soon as we arrived with Lieutenant Diller, Sergeant Fudge yelled out,

"Cell 5! Cell 5!" pointing in the direction of the cell.

Officer Slick was still inside the officer's station, combing his hair and reading the newspaper as if this was a regular occurrence. Lieutenant Diller stopped us from entering and stated,

"Guys, we got a cutter!"

This particular inmate was prohibited from having a razor due to his continual tendency to cut himself from past incarcerations. Apparently, another inmate gave him a razor, which he took apart and used to slice himself after he locked himself in his cell with his unwilling cellmate. There was so much blood on the floor it was leaking out from under the cell door and into the dayroom for other inmates to see.

Officer Slick was the main officer who found inmate Poole cutting himself when he saw blood leaking underneath the cell door. As Slick looked inside the cell, inmate Poole's cellmate was seen curled up in a ball in the corner of his bunk as the cutter cut his wrists from the wrist to his elbow, bleeding all over the floor, the toilet, and drawing on the walls with his own blood. Lieutenant Diller looked into the cell as the cutter continued to slice at his arms.

Lieutenant Diller quickly went to the side of the door with his back to the wall, looking up at the ceiling, stating,

"I can't look."

He called control to contact an ambulance for transport to the local hospital when he started sweating profusely. He suddenly appeared very flushed, almost white in the face.

"Lieutenant are you ok?" asked Dean.

He responded,

"No, not really, Dean."

Officer Dean worked Unit 3, so she knew the inmate in question from another floor.

"Captain, do you mind if I talk to him?" asked Dean.

74

The Captain responded,

"You can try, Dean! I'm staying right here!"

as he wiped the dripping sweat from his forehead. Officer Johnston ran towards the unit sliding doors, to direct the ambulance crew, as soon as they arrived.

Officer Dean tried to get the cutter's attention by distracting him,

"Sir, remember me? I work this unit on occasion."

Mr. Poole replied,

"Yes, Dean, I know you, but I started this and now the voices told me to finish it."

He then sliced his throat open. The blood started to squirt out on the small, dirty cell window. As the blood squirted on the window, Officer Dean continued to distract Mr. Poole by getting him to look at the floor, stating,

"Mr. Poole, please stop; you are getting weak from blood loss, just look at the floor! You are going to slip and fall out! Please stop!"

Mr. Poole stated,

"Ms, I started this, now I have to finish the job."

At that point, Officer Dean observed Mr. Poole appear to swallow the razor blade.

"He appeared to swallow the razor blade, Lieutenant!"

Officer Dean stated to the inmate,

"Please stop before you pass out from the loss of blood!"

Dean watched him look at the floor as he started to slip on his own blood. The cellmate was covering his eyes, rocking back and forth from seeing the traumatic scene taking place right in front of him.

The special team showed up, in their protective gear, on the unit to assist in getting him out of the cell without incident. Officer Dean asked Mr. Poole if he could please turn around so we could get him the help he needs. Surprisingly, Mr. Poole did turn around, as the team gave the camera to the Lieutenant to record the event. The Lieutenant gave the camera back to Dean to record the cell extraction. The Lieutenant stated,

"Dean, you got this."

Mr. Poole was ready to be cuffed as the team opened the trap door. As both team members grabbed a wrist to apply the handcuffs, they realized Mr. Poole also cut all the way around his wrists, so when they started placing the handcuffs on, the skin around his wrists peeled down onto his hands. One of the special team members started gagging profusely at the sight of this. Not only do the smells of blood get to you, but also what you see, which you can never unsee again. That image still sticks in Dean's head even to this day.

As Officer Johnston arrived back on the unit with the ambulance crew and a nurse, the team struggled to keep it together. The cell door opened, and the inmate cutter was told to back out of the cell slowly. Mr. Poole was getting extremely dizzy due to the loss of blood. As Dean continued to videotape the extraction, the special team had the inmate cutter sit at a table close by before he fell out. This inmate was massive, approximately 300 lbs easy.

This event was all going down in front of many spectators, and other inmates. A few started yelling out of their cell doors,

"Man, how long is this going to take! I'm missing my show right now! Wow, that's a lot of blood, man! I think I'm going to get sick looking at that!"

The ambulance crew told Mr. Poole they would have to cut off his jumpsuit to help him with his injuries. Mr. Poole stated,

"Do what you gotta do, man. I'm not feeling so hot right now!"

The ambulance crew proceeded to cut off his jumpsuit in the center as his arms were cuffed behind his back. The nurse started placing pressure on his neck and arm wounds, wrapping in gauze, as the ambulance crew took vitals. Lieutenant Diller, still on the unit, was not looking at the scene due to his gagging and white complexion. Dean was still videotaping the scene while the ambulance crew wrapped up his other wounds, including his neck.

Mr. Poole was completely naked, sitting on a cold, steel dayroom stool, connected to a table, which was bolted to the floor. The special team and ambulance crew assisted Mr. Poole to the gurney for the ride to the hospital. As the special team secured Mr. Poole to the gurney, they made sure he wasn't going anywhere. However, they needed to get the transport bag from intake before they left the intake area with the ambulance crew.

As they left, Lieutenant Diller asked for the camera from Dean, stating

"Good job keeping it together!" then left with the crew.

Dean was left looking at the huge bloody mess from the cell to the dayroom area. She walked over to cell 5 asking if the cellmate was ok. He stated he was extremely appreciative his cellmate didn't hurt him. Dean asked him if he was ok to step out so we could clean up the cell. He stated,

"Sure."

Sergeant Fudge asked the inmate if he needed to see mental health on the unit as his office was located right on the unit, over the loudspeaker. He stated,

"It can't hurt me none."

Then proceeded to his office while Dean assisted the inmate swamper with the clean-up.

Officer Slick decided to go home sick, so Officer Dean was left to work on this unit until a fill-in came in to replace her. The inmate swamper was let out of his cell and proceeded to fill a mop bucket of water with a cleaning solution in it to start the clean-up process. As he came closer to the cell, he stated,

"Looks like a crime scene here with all of this blood," Dean replied,

"Sure, does don't it"as she handed him some gloves.

Dean gloved up also as she asked if he had another mop bucket. The inmate swamper asked,

"You gonna help out, Officer?" Dean stated,

"I'm not going to have you clean-up a mess if I'm not willing to help clean it up too."

The inmate swamper was very appreciative.

Later that day, before the shift ended, the special team members and the escorts involved with the incident on unit 3 were called down to attend a debriefing on Mr. Poole. Since Lieutenant Diller also went home sick, Captain Munch conducted the debriefing with staff. As the group entered the room, an officer, who was in intake, was drawing a picture of the inmate's face on the board, placing raccoon markings under his eyes just like Mr. Poole did to himself as if this was supposed to be funny. Captain Munch asked if any of us needed to see someone for what we just witnessed. Most everyone stated,

"No."

As the room was emptying, I stated,

"Is that what you call a debriefing?"

The Captain stated,

"Well, yeah. You have a problem with that Dean?"

Dean responded, "So making fun of someone with a mental illness is supposed to be funny to you?" The Captain replied,

"Well, did it help?"

Dean stated,

"No, it just made me mad that you find serious situations, such as this, funny! I find no humor in making fun of people with serious mental health issues!"

Officer Dean left without saying another word.

This traumatic event was the first of many more to be seen by Officer Dean during her time working for the institution. People with serious mental health issues need help, not reduced to a joke or made into a laughable event, especially for those who are affected by schizophrenia. This is a serious mental health condition which needs to be taken care of in the most respectful manner for not only the person suffering but also the family who must care for the individual family member.

Where's the Light Bulb?

Officer Dean was working on the segregation unit on a day a light bulb went missing in one of the strip cages, where two officers placed a new inmate from intake.

Apparently, he threatened the intake Captain and tried to spit at him but missed. He was then double escorted to the segregation floor to be placed in a clear room, per the psychologist on duty. The inmate refused to strip out of his clothes while in the cage, even though he was attached to the cell door by a leather tether. The staff had to wait for a Captain or Lieutenant to arrive on the unit to see if he could talk him into cooperating with the staff.

This was the first time Officer Dean had to work with Sergeant Peckel on the segregation unit. He was this muscle-bound guy with a neck bigger than his head. Any person could tell he must be on steroids or something due to his face being covered in acne and his quickness to anger. Dean worked with him another time when he was screaming at a captain to write Dean up for insubordination. However, Dean was commended on doing the right things with that inmate who, it turned out, had contracted MRSA. Apparently, Sgt. Peckel would leave the unit frequently to wander the building, flirting with other female officers, as Dean had observed prior to working with him. Today, he left the unit to flirt with staff across the hall as Dean held down the unit. Dean thought it pissed him off that she didn't give him the time of day; just did her job. Sergeant Peckel also had his buddy working with him. The inmates called the other officer.

"Big Shit"

because he was all shit and had no brains, just like Sgt. Peckel. Big Shit was hiding in the bathroom for the past hour while Dean contacted a Captain to respond to segregation. Captain Mac was on today, and he quickly responded over the radio; he was en route as the escort staff waited patiently in the hallway of segregation. Sgt. Peckel showed up asking why the escort officers were waiting for Captain Mac when HE could get the inmate to cooperate.

Meanwhile, when staff was not watching the inmate in the cage, the inmate was able to break the light bulb located at the top of the cage and ate the broken pieces. Then Sgt. Peckel shows up, grabs the leather tether the inmate was still attached to, then yells toward the officer bubble stating,

"You want to see a hero, Dean? This is being a hero!"

He then pulls the tether so hard the inmate's arm appears as if it was yanked from his socket in one swift move. One of the escort officers stated,

"Look, he's trying to show off for the new female officer."

The other officers were laughing as if this was an act of bravery on the part of Sgt. Peckel. This was pure abuse.

Now, Officer Dean was also not aware the inmate had eaten the light bulb due to not being able to see inside the cage from how the officer's station was positioned as Captain Mac arrived on theunit. Sgt. Peckel had just opened the cuffs on the leather tether belt, so now the inmate was sitting on shards of glass. He was still chewing on the glass as he continued to place more pieces in his mouth. Captain Mac disliked Sgt. Peckel's attitude, which Dean did not know. Captain Mac saw the inmate and asked him what he was chewing on. The inmate apparently smiled with bloody teeth, continuing to chew on the glass. Sgt. Peckel stated,

"I just got him to cooperate with me by taking off the tether."

Captain Mac was furious, stating,

"Did you not see he broke the light bulb from the cage, and apparently, he's chewing on the glass, Peckel?"

Sgt. Peckel responded,

"He must have just done that right before you came on the unit, Captain."

At this point, Captain Mac asked the inmate if he would be so kind as to allow him to be escorted to a better cell after he got cleaned up. Surprisingly, the inmate did cooperate and allowed Captain Mac to tether him and allow the escort officers to move him to another cell. As the inmate got up off the floor, he had shards of glass stuck in his backside and feet due to not being given shoes while in intake. Captain Mac contacted a nurse to have the shards taken out and check the inmate's well-being. The inmate cooperated with staff and had the shards removed by the nurse while in segregation, with officer's present.

Captain Mac had a discussion with Sgt. Peckel about the directive and rule violations regarding removal of the tether before a Captain is on the unit. Meanwhile, the inmate asked for a complaint form from staff during chow due to his arm seriously hurting.

"Here you go, Sir, only if you promise not to eat the paperwork, ok? The inmate's response,

"I promise, madam." with a smile

Chapter 8
The Mail Room Diaries

Officer Dean worked with a variety of units throughout her tenure at MSDF. One of those areas worked was the notorious mail room. The mail room was an overwhelming small room full of received or sending out of mail, sort of like fitting a ten-pound bag of apples into a bag which could only hold about three pounds at any given time. There were only two mail room staff who had the ungodly task of going through all the received mail into the institution. Any mail going out was read unless it was considered legal communications. Those inmates who sent mail to their loved/ liked ones or another institution were required to be read due to threats of violence, gang communications, or any other suspect mail. Some of those letters, for example, which were written in another language, needed to be translated from that language to English, which was done by on-site translators. Nothing was missed through these communications. Often, mail was intercepted, which contained threats of violence, possible hits on witnesses, or threats of self-injury, needed immediate attention. At times, those threats involved more charges such as witness tampering, gang hits, or mental health interventions. If you only knew what was sent into an institution, you would never want to touch another piece of mail again, unless you were wearing rubber gloves.

One day, Officer Dean was ordered to assist the mailroom staff due to one officer calling in sick. This was her first time working in this capacity. One she would never forget. With bare hands, Dean started opening the mail with a machine which opened all the envelopes from a pile of non-legal mail, which was separated by the other officer. As Dean separated the mail per unit in piles, both officers together started opening the envelopes to quickly read them. Now, to describe the mailroom walls. The mailroom officers set up a wall of shame. These were photos the inmates were not allowed to see due to exposed lady bits or other depictions described in the DOC policy. Yes, lady bits were prohibited from being seen by the inmates. The inmates were sent a letter stating the mailroom received prohibited photos and given the option to either pay to return the photo, or have it destroyed. Those photos, which were not to be returned, but destroyed, somehow ended up hanging on the wall of shame as examples to other officers to abide by policy by not sending photos like those posted, to inmates. These photos either depicted gang signs, death threats, gang or drug paraphernalia, harm to children, vulnerable elderly, or animals, and, last but not least, lady bits. On occasion, items will be sent in which need to be returned if they did not come from an approved source, such as a direct mailing from an approved book store or approved religious material.

Well, because this was Dean's first day in the mailroom, it happened to be packed with mail. The officers had to work hard to get the mail read and organized by floor and unit. As Officer Dean walked in, the other officer yelled, "Watch yourself so you don't trip on anything, dear!" As Dean maneuvered around the numerous boxes of mail, between incoming and outgoing mail, she quickly noticed an array of photos posted on the Wall of Shame. This wall contained numerous pictures a mother or grandmother would never approve of. In fact, some were downright, wrong on so many levels. Unfortunately, when photos are approved without exposing lady bits, these ladies don't understand their photos are passed around like a bag of chips. Every inmate is going to see those pictures due to the bragging rights of it's owner. Some may want this persons address or even swipe the address to write a letter to this woman. This is called,

"Fishing."

One of the ways inmates try to solicit a vulnerable woman to get her to send in money to place on their books or account. The inmates who do this, actually solicit several women at a time. The inmate says the right things to woo the unsuspecting woman before asking her for money. Some inmates who have had their cells randomly searched or cleaned out due to moving the individual to segregation, would be corresponding to several women at a time. Each of these women would be sending money to the inmate so he had money to purchase commissary.

The women never catch on unless they happen to arrive at the same time for visits.

One instance, Officer Dean happened to be working in the lobby when three different women arrived to see one male inmate. One had a child in tow, and the other two knew each other. As one came to the counter with her ID in hand asking to see Mr. Johnson, the lady behind her asked for Mr. Johnson as well. They both looked at each other asking what Mr. Johnson's first name was. One lady loudly stated,

"William Johnson? You here for a William Johnson? Must be two William Johnson's up in here!"

Then the third lady with the child stated,

"You here to see a William Johnson? You best not be here to see my man! You best be a sister or cousin, bitches!"

As she raised her hand in the air. That's when it went down in the lobby. Officer Dean and Sgt. Monroe had to call for back up and the city police department to make a few arrests that day. There were broken nails, blood, parts of a weave, and a bottle for the little boy left behind after the scuffle. Fortunately, two out of the three women left behind their ID's during the brawl and a lot of paperwork to be completed. All that fighting over a man who was scamming them all. It wasn't the first time, nor the last time Dean would see such a clash of women fighting over someone incarcerated.

As Dean and the other mailroom officer started to open and read the numerous letters and cards sent in by loved or liked ones. Dean noticed many smelled of perfumes sprayed on them, some had hair clippings, lipstick marks, and such. The other mailroom officer quickly stated,

"Baby, don't touch anything suspicious!"

Dean noticed the other mailroom officer eating out of a bag of chips and not wearing gloves, so she didn't think she had too either. So, she went about her business opening the letters piled by her by the other officer to read. The mailroom officer then stated,

"These piles ain't goin to get done by themselves, girl! Pull up a chair and start reading!"

Officer Dean grabbed a chair, sat down, then started opening the many envelopes laying in piles on the big table. She decided to pick floor 4, Unit 4A. This was a program unit for those needing a program required by the state probation and parole officers according to the inmates offense. The social workers taught anger management, addiction groups, parenting, domestic violence and such.

As Officer Dean started opening a few envelopes, she came upon an envelope that appeared to have candy wrapped in little red wrappings, similar to tiny strawberry candies. Dean grabbed one of these by the wrapper, holding it in the air asking the mailroom officer,

"Look at this!"

The mailroom officer quickly stated,

"Girl, What floor are those being sent to?"

Dean quickly replied,

"Unit 4A, why"? The mailroom officer then quickly stated, "Dean, drop it!"

Officer Dean dropped that wrapped candy so quick as if it had a spider on it, yelling

"EEEK!"

The mailroom officer stated,

"Girl, there is a woman sending in her shit wrapped in little candy wrappers."

As Dean had this look on her face in disgust, she quickly headed to the nearest bathroom to wash her hands, so viciously, she got her crisp uniform sleeves all wet with soap and water. Mind you, this is the first time Dean worked in the mailroom. After that incident, gloves were a required part of this job.

Several days later, Officer Dean was sent to unit 4A to relieve a sick officer who was going home that day. As she placed her backpack on the floor, inside the officer's station of this open unit, an inmate came up to desk asking Dean if he could switch cells due to his cellmate. Dean asked what the problem was. The inmate stated,

"I just used the toilet and my cellmate just told me to not flush the toilet and leave the cell."

Dean asked him which cell he was in? The inmate stated,

"It's cell 15, right over there."

As he pointed in the direction of the cell.

Officer Dean bent over the counter of the officer station and looked in the direction of the cell, as the cell door was open, she saw, what appeared to be, a man kneeling in front of the steel toilet with his face inside the bowl of that toilet. His hands were gripping the side of that toilet as if he was washing his face inside the toilet bowl. Officer Dean watched this inmate slowly get up off his knees from kneeling on the floor, face dripping of God knows what, then go wash his face in the sink of that cell. With the cellmate still standing in front of the officer, the inmate stated,

"See, he's some sick dude, Ms. Can you please move me out of that cell, officer, please!"

Dean asked the Sargent on the unit if she could move the cellmate into an available open cell due to strangely sick behavior of the other inmate. While the cellmate was told to have a seat in the dayroom, Dean shared what she just observed the guy doing in that toilet. Dean got the attention of the Sargent really quick. As both officers discussed what was just observed, the inmate with the poop fetish walked up to the officer's desk asking if he has a visitor yet. This man was a very nice-looking guy with fancy, expensive, shaded glasses on, wearing a perfect, unblemished smile. Dean almost choked on her own saliva. Apparently, the

Sargent hired him to be the new floor swamper after the other swamper was informed of his departure that very day. Officer Dean asked,

"Sir, what is your name, please?"

When he stated his name, Officer Dean made the immediate connection to the shitty candy wrappers.

You Can't make this shit up. No pun intended.

Chapter 9
Shenanigans and Tomfoolery

There were many times, Officer Dean just shook her head in disbelief at the behavior of fellow staff and inmates. She worked on the diabetic unit, 7B with Sargent Benson one day. He was a no-nonsense kind of person who also wanted to do the right thing regarding inmates and the many staff he worked with. He happened to be one of officer Dean's favorite Sergeants to work with due to the fact he really appreciated Dean's style and approach to working with the inmates on this particular unit. Not one person fell out during their shift due to the diligence and understanding of diabetic issues Officer Dean read about. She educated herself in the understanding of this disease and how to familiarize herself to the signals of diabetic crisis at her local library.

On this particular day, she followed her routine of standing count at 0615, then onto taking care of the diabetic gentlemen before breakfast arrived. She forgot to place her gloves on since she could get those inside the medical room where she monitored the diabetic blood sugar numbers and issued syringes to those who needed insulin. She allowed two gentlemen at one time into the medical room to check their blood sugar on their personal monitors. As she unlocked the syringe drawer, she reached into the drawer to grab the syringes, without looking and discovered they were splattered with blood. All the syringes had blood splattered all over the wrappings. She quickly dropped the syringes back into the drawer and washed her hands. She needed to call a nurse to the unit to bring up a package of new needles to distribute. In the meantime, she had the inmates wait until the nurse arrived before she continued. Officer Dean did not want those who had already compromised health to come in contact with what was left inside that drawer, covered in blood. The nurse came pretty quickly as she was on the other side of the hallway, finishing with unit 7C and 7D.

After Officer Dean washed her hands, she went to find her size gloves, but they were also gone, so she grabbed any size available so she could count how many syringes were in the drawer. The previous shift either miscounted or used one for an inmate and did not inform anyone. The last count recorded was 18, but only 17 were in the drawer. She called the Sargent as he was opening the door for the nurse, to inform him what occurred and what was missing. He stated one inmate was given insulin during the night, however, that syringe was not counted for in the logbook. The inmate in question overheard the conversation and verified he was in need of insulin during the night due to not being given a snack bag. Snack bags were given to those who needed to have natural sugar in case they felt low during the night.

The nurse came into the medical room and replaced the dirty syringes with new ones. She stated,

"Why would anyone do that, Dean!"

as the nurse handed a new pack of syringes to Dean.

"I have given up trying to figure that one out, Patty!" Patty, the nurse, decided to stay as Dean took care of the diabetic inmates, then Nurse Patty distributed the numerous regular morning medications while she was on the unit. Dean enjoyed working with Nurse Patty. Anytime Dean had a question about health issues or inmate complaint, she would know it was a serious situation and would always come back up to the unit to check. Somebody locked that drawer, knowing blood was splattered all over those syringes and it was either an officer or a nurse.

"What the heck!"

Several months later there was an emergency on 7B as Officer Dean was again assigned to work that unit. Sgt. Peckel was the Sgt. On the unit. Dean hated working with this guy. He didn't care about anyone on these units except his sick way of flirting with female staff. Anyway, Dean had an inmate come up to her in distress. He was one of the diabetics on the unit. He appeared clammy, sweating profusely, and shaky. The inmate, Mr. Leanard, came up to the officer station window to ask Sgt. Peckel if someone could test his blood sugar because he was not feeling well. Sgt. Peckel yelled at Mr. Leanard stating,

"Get your fucken hands off my window, you nappy headed mother fucker!"

Now, Officer Dean overheard the yelling from the Sgt. On the other side of the unit where Dean was working. Dean hated being in the bubble with Sgt. Peckel. He was always trying to flirt or touch her, so Dean stayed out on the unit the entire day with the inmates. Since Dean overheard Sgt. Peckel screaming profanity-laced obscenities to Mr. Leanard, she went through the bathroom door to the other side of the unit. The unit officer, Big Shit, was off the unit, usually in his favorite place, in the hallway bathroom. Dean didn't care if it was almost time for shift change, Dean went over to the other side and immediately noticed he really was not feeling well. Dean popped open the medical room and got Mr. Leanard's kit with his blood sugar meter and checked with Mr. Leanard. Mr. Leanard's blood sugar was at 40. Dean stated,

"Shit"!

Dean had Mr. Leanard sit on a chair in the medical room as she unlocked the drawers to get the sugar tabs out and gave Mr. Leanard two to start with. While she called Sgt. Peckel to inform him about Mr. Leanard's condition, Sgt. Peckel stated,

"Fuck him!"

hanging up on Dean. Dean then contacted nursing staff, and a nurse came right up to check on Mr. Leanard, bringing an apple and some peanut butter and two milks. Dean stayed with Mr. Leanard until he was ok'ed by the nurse to go back to his room. Sgt. Peckel was long gone at that point. He was a terrible Sgt.

Secret Hiding Spot

Officer Dean was assigned to assist Sgt. Hopper on the 6th floor, Unit 6C, a regular population unit during a lice infestation. She was to stay inside the officer's station with Sgt. Hopper while the other officers were collecting all the bedding and clothing from the inmates. Everyone had to shower with the lice shampoo and soap again, then assigned new bedding and clothing. During this time, Officer Dean was opening and closing cell doors and monitoring the dayroom from inside the officer station when an inmate came to the officer station trap. The inmate stated,

"Excuse me officer, I swear to God I heard people having sex outside of my back wall last night."

Officer Dean didn't know what to say since some inmates with mental health issues may hear things we don't, or it could have been someone in a dream state, who knows. He went on to describe where his head was when he was hearing these sounds.

"The top of my head is facing the back wall of my cell; it was so loud I had to switch sides where my head was closer to the cell door."

All Dean could say was,

"I'll check it out, Sir. OK?"

He seemed to be satisfied with the answer she gave him. At first, she thought it could be fellow inmates, he may have been dreaming or something else. Sgt. Hopper stated,

"He's crazy Dean. Don't listen to him."

Later that day after the entire unit was finished with showers, bedding and clothing exchanges, she was relieved by the officer on the floor and ordered to report to the control center.

The control center assigned Officer Dean a list of toilets, which had to be reset, along with specific floors and units. She was handed the special keys which gave access to these areas as she observed another officer show her once several months prior. This officer knew the ins and outs of the institution and all the hiding places, apparently. The list included floors 4 through 7, and which unit on each side with the specific cell which needed to be reset. Resetting a toilet meant the toilet was either plugged with garbage/ or something an inmate was trying to hide by flushing it down the toilet, plugged with fecal matter, or was just plugged by overuse.

As Dean entered each corridor behind the cell walls, where the reset buttons were for each toilet, she observed these spaces were filled with old, outdated equipment. There were old chairs, desks, stacks of unused books, and more used junk. As she proceeded through these corridors, resetting the toilets so they could flush, she would contact the sergeant on every floor to have the inmates flush the toilets to make sure they worked. As soon as she heard the toilet flush successfully, she would move on to the next toilet or floor.

Officer Dean had one toilet to reset on the 6th floor, the floor she was just on assisting with the lice outbreak. As she opened the corridor door and walked in, she observed the numerous out-of-date office equipment lined up alongside the walls on the left and to the right were the walls with the reset switches for the numerous toilets. As she walked farther in that space, there was a clearing of floor space with yellow inmate clothing lying on the floor and what appeared to be, a used rubber laying nearby. It just so happened the inmate who reported hearing sounds of someone having sex, was not made-up in his head after all. This mess was in close proximity of the cell in question. Dean radioed Sgt. Hopper to have the inmate flush his toilet as she reset it. The inmate was in his cell at the time and heard Officer Dean behind the cell wall. He stated,

"I can hear you back there Officer!"

as he flushed his toilet. Dean stated,

"Is your toilet working, Sir?"

He responded,

"Yes, thank you, Officer!"

She took the inmate clothing, which consisted of two yellow tops and three bottom pants and a pillow, out of the corridor and deposited it in the dirty pile on unit 6C, informing Sgt. Hopper what she found directly behind the cell where the inmate reported what he heard. Sgt. Hopper just stated,

"WTF, Dean!"

Seriously? As Officer Dean returned to the control area to leave for the day, the regular officer who resets toilets, was in the front lobby with another female officer. As Dean walked by them both, he was straightening his hair with his comb as she was buttoning her top button on her shirt. Gross.

Locked in a Cell

Dean was assigned to work with Sgt. Peckel and Officer Big Shit on the 9th floor, unit 9A and B. Sgt. Peckel was not a good sergeant. In fact, other officers hated working with this clown due to aggravating inmates all the time. Dean thought he appeared to be the kid at school who was bullied by others then turned into an adult on a mission to make everyone's lives miserable because of it. His friend, Big Shit was just a lazy guy, big and brawny, who followed everything his friend Peckel told him to do. Big Shit would disappear for an hour using the bathroom, would not watch his unit, and would sleep in the officer's station with his

DOC hat covering his eyes. Big Shit would prop his chair against the wall, cross his arms and just nap while Sgt. Peckel wandered the institution hitting on all of the female staff.

Officer Dean was not a fan of his and he knew it. An inmate would come to the officer station window asking for a slip for the doctor or dentist and Sgt. Peckel would scream across the officer station,

"Get the Fuck away from my window you nappy headed freak!"

Dean would just say to the inmate,

"I'll bring some out with me, ok, Sir?"

Sometimes, the inmate would scream back at Sgt. Peckel,

"I'm talking to this female officer and not your funky ass!"

Sometimes, the inmate would write up a complaint, and sometimes, Sgt. Peckel would write up a ticket for disrespect to the inmate just because he took it personally. Either way, the day was always made harder working with those two characters, hmm, co-workers.

Today was the day Officer Dean would experience something she would never forget. Sgt. Peckel screamed at an inmate who always gave it back verbally, saying it must have touched a nerve. In the academy, we are told never to take things personally regarding what is said to us on a daily basis. We are always the targets even though we did not arrest anyone, sentence anyone, or determine the fate of anyone who becomes incarcerated. We are there to not only keep order but to make sure everyone is taken care of regarding clean clothing, safety, meals, medical emergencies, report possible mental health issues, distribute laundry and linens, mail, canteen distribution, medications, toilet paper, you get the picture.

Sgt. Peckel decided to rip apart this inmate's cell one day, unbeknownst to Officer Dean, then recruited Officer Big Shit to assist him in his efforts after the noon count. He ordered Dean to stay inside the officer station while they did rounds then to let the lower tier out for dayroom. So, Officer Dean opened the officer station door, allowed the sergeant and officer out, and then proceeded to open the pod door to Officer Dean's unit to do rounds. As the lower tier was allowed out for dayroom, Officer Dean observed her co-workers make a beeline to the inmate cell. Sgt. Peckel had a beef with. As Sgt. Peckel ordered the two inmates out of the cell and into the dayroom, Sgt. Peckel and Officer Big Shit proceeded to enter this cell. Together they started ripping apart all the bedding, property, and toiletries while the inmates looked on.

The inmates started to complain about what the officers were doing as Sgt. Peckel proceeded to dump two fruit cups he found into the sink and splatter the cell with them. Sgt. Peckel accused Dean of not doing better cell searches for contraband, which Dean always did. Dean also was told by Sgt. Peckel to write incident reports on the inmates when she found any contraband. Dean was informed by a senior officer who collected the daily reports, that she writes up more incident reports than others instead of learning how to talk to inmates. This senior officer did not know when she was forced to work with Sgt. Peckle, he was telling her to write up the inmates because HE had the problem of not communicating properly to inmates. Dean learned over time to just talk to the inmates on her units instead of writing so many incident reports. A valuable lesson learned.

Something interesting happened at that moment; as all the inmates in the dayroom observed this event happening, one inmate proceeded to run up to the cell door both, Sgt. Peckle and Big Shit were in at the time. The inmate quickly slammed it shut, locking Sgt. Peckel and

Officer Big Shit inside. This inmate ran to the gym area and locked the gym door to make it appear he had nothing to do with it because it locked him and others inside. Officer Dean just savored this moment for a few seconds before contacting control. She ordered everyone to return to their cells then contacted control to report the incident.

Before the team arrived, the two inmates who resided in the cell which was being ripped apart by both the officers, were ordered by Officer Dean to the other side of the dayroom and have a seat. Both inmates did just what Officer Dean told them to do.

As Captain Mac arrived with the entire team of eight officers, he observed Sgt. Peckel and Officer Big Shit locked inside the cell as the team handcuffed the two inmates who belonged in that cell while the other officers secured all the lower-tier cell doors. Captain Mac walked up to the cell which held Sgt. Peckel and Officer Big Shit then motioned to have Officer Dean open the cell door to allow them out. Sgt. Peckel and Officer Big Shit marched to the pod door with the captain and then entered the officer station. Captain Mac laid into both, stating,

"What the hell were you both doing inside a cell"?

Sgt. Peckel stated,

"We were just doing a cell search!"

Captain Mac replied,

"You know the policy is to have one person conduct a search while the other officer stays outside the cell door! Isn't this the third time you've been locked inside a cell, Peckel!"

As this back-and-forth ass-chewing continued, Officer Dean was writing a conduct report on the inmate who slammed the cell door, locking them inside. Captain Mac stated,

"Dean, did you see who did it!"

Officer Dean responded,

"Yes, Sir and here is the ticket. I'll pack up his property as soon as you have him off the unit, Captain!"

The captain proceeded to yell at Sgt. Peckel stating,

"You're lucky she observed who did this, Peckel! I want to see you and Big Shit in my office after this shift!"

As the Captain left the officer station with the ticket in hand, he directed the team to uncuff the two inmates whose cell was torn apart by the officer and Sgt. He directed Officer Dean to open the gym door to retrieve the inmate responsible for closing the cell door on Sgt. Peckel and Officer Big Shit. The team grabbed and cuffed the inmate in the gym as the inmate was overheard stating,

"But I was locked in the gym! How could I be responsible! Man, this is some fucked up shit!"

Captain Mac waved at Officer Dean as they escorted the inmate to Segregation. The dayroom was now open. Sgt. Peckel took his hat off, slammed it to the floor angrily stating,

"Fuck those inmates! How could this fucken happen again!"

Maybe it was your wonderful personality.

Hooch Anyone?

There comes a time when a few inmates get the bright idea to create what we would call,

"Hooch."

A substance so revolting and toxic it could make a person very sick and or, cause death.

Today was no different. Addictions to alcohol play a huge role in making hooch in prison. Officer Dean was sitting out on a unit, a unit she had never worked on in the past. Within an hour, she observed a hired inmate swamper get a container down from a shelf inside the swamper closet,then sit close to the container. He was observed placing a few sugar packets into the container. As she watched him stir the mixture, she noticed the other swamper trying to distract her attention away from what she was witnessing. The inmate swamper, who was stirring the mixture, had his back facing Officer Dean. She then stood up and proceeded to the swamper closet to see what the inmate swamper had. She walked up as the other swamper gave his partner a heads-up. It was too late.

Officer Dean was standing right behind the inmate swamper as he quickly stood up, turning to look right at her. She quickly stated, "What are you doing, Cones?" He didn't know what to say. The room had a strong odor emitting from it, almost inebriating all by itself. Inmate Cones begged Officer Dean to not report it. She had to report this incident, no if's, and's, or but's. It was so strong she started to get a whiff of this mixture as she picked it up off the floor, placed a cover on it, then walked it to the officer station. As she brought this container into the small officer station and closed the door, the officers were stunned from their naps. The Sargent stated,

"So, what is this Dean?"

condescendingly, as he rocked in his tattered chair, crossing his fingers. She replied,

"Well Sgt. this is hooch, and it was found in YOUR swamper closet, one of your workers was mixing it when I caught him. The other swamper was also involved."

The Sgt. replied,

"I highly doubt this is hooch. We run a tight ship on this unit and no female officer is going to tell me what goes on my unit,"

This was not the first time Officer Dean found hooch. She remembers there had been several inmates who drank hooch they made and ended up in the hospital because of it.

As the Sgt. snapped the lid off of this concoction, the officer station instantly filled up with intoxicating fumes that were extremely strong. As the Sgt. started coughing along with the other officers, the Sgt. called the captain's office to report what Officer Dean found. The captain could not believe it, so he ordered one of the officers to bring it to the captain's office for verification. Meanwhile, everyone was ordered to their bunks as Officer Dean started to fill out two conduct reports on both inmate swampers.

Apparently, the Captain on duty also didn't believe it was hooch until the intoxicating substance filled their office area also. Within minutes, there was a huge team formed which entered the unit. The two swampers were handcuffed, asked why they were making hooch knowing it was against the rules, which could have had a devastating effect on whomever drank such a concoction. The offenders were roughly handled right in front of Dean. The officers slammed one inmate against the wall so hard, spit flew right out of his mouth, right in front of Dean, then marched off the unit.

As they were marched off the unit, the main swamper turned to look at Officer Dean, then was quickly grabbed by the back of his neck and turned away from looking back at her. She had both conduct reports done and sent along with the captain. The male officers on the unit in question and the Sgt. were pissed because it was happening right under their noses and found by a female officer they disliked.

People will do things right in front of your face. You must be vigilant enough to pay attention to your surroundings.

Broken Jaw

Remember in Chapter 1, where two officers identified as Officer Stanke and Officer Dough were talked about messing with inmate property by allegedly dumping the inmate's lotion all over his property and left for Officer Dean to clean up. Sgt. Benson was livid by the behavior of these two officers. The inmate in question was Mr. Peabody, Peabody was an active inmate on the unit as if he may appear to have symptoms of ADHD, just could not sit still. He either walked around the unit repetitively, would talk to everyone on the unit, he would be in and out of the unit gym, similar to a kid who just ate a whole box of little Debbie cakes. Mr. Peabody never gave Dean a problem, even if she had to correct him, he did as told, but was just very active in nature.

It was his property box, which was later found out after Officer Dean cleaned off all the lotion from his photos, legal work and hygiene items. Apparently, four days prior, Dean left the unit to go home and had four days off when the next shift came on the unit after her. The officers did not like Mr. Peabody and had him taken to segregation because he would not listen to them, supposedly. It was reported to Dean Mr. Peabody asked the officers to lock up his property because he didn't want his cellmate to steal his hygiene. The officers told him to shut the fuck up, as he was cuffed behind his back. Mr. Peabody continued to ask the officers to lock his stuff up. As he was escorted by a Lieutenant and two officers to segregation, he was taken into the elevator and beaten up so badly because he wanted his property locked up and told to shut the fuck up several times but continued to protest. He ended up in segregation and was offered medical due to "Falling down" in the elevator. He refused. Mr. Peabody was in segregation for 21 days for whatever offense he violated.

After he was returned to unit 7B, Officer Dean was assigned to work on unit 7B and was not aware he was even back on the unit. When Officer Dean did the morning count, she realized he was back on the same unit, but this time something was off. Mr. Peabody looked thinner and was lying in his bed, not the active, chipper person she was used to. He was facing the wall of his bunk when his new cellmate came out and shared with Dean there was something wrong with his cellmate. At that point, Dean realized it was Mr. Peabody. Dean stated,

"I see you are finally back on the unit, what is going on. You don't seem like the same person I saw almost a month ago".

As Mr. Peabody turned to look at Dean, Dean observed Mr. Peabody's face appeared swollen. He stated,

"Ms. Dean, I'm so glad to see you. They put me in the hole for no reason. Right after you left that one day. All I said to them was I wanted my property locked up because I was afraid my stuff would go missing, and they continued to tell me to shut the fuck up."

Mr. Peabody stated,

"My face really hurts, and I haven't eaten much."

Dean asked if he was willing to be seen by the doctor. Mr. Peabody stated,

"Yes, I don't know what is wrong with my face. You know they beat me up in the elevator, right?"

Dean was stunned to hear of this. It would almost be unbelievable to accuse officers of doing such behavior in the company of a Lieutenant. Dean called the Health Services Unit to see if he could be seen today due to what she suspected to be some sort of facial injury which prevented him from not eating. The HSU escort later came up to get him so he could be seen.

Anytime Dean called the HSU unit at the institution, the nursing staff and doctor knew it was necessary to follow up. Dean developed this connection over time because she had been right every time, with the MRSA, with the hooch, and with the man dragging his leg. So, it must have been Mr. Peabody's lucky day. Thursdays were the only day of the week when the medical staff had an X-ray there for anything needed to be addressed by other inmates reporting any injuries or other illnesses. Mr. Peabody was then X-rayed and was informed of what was going on with his face. Upon his return to the unit, Mr. Peabody informed Dean what exactly happened. He stated,

"They took me to that elevator, Ms. Dean and they beat me up. My hands were cuffed behind my back. I think they knew they hurt me real bad when my mouth was bleeding. My face didn't feel right and now I know what they did. My jaw is broken on both sides, Ms."

After Mr. Peabody informed me of this, it was hard to take in. I returned to the unit bubble and just sat there until Lieutenant Koop arrived on the unit just to do his rounds or whatever. What came out of his mouth next was so disturbing I reacted. I have never told someone off in a leadership position before, so this was uncharted territory for Dean. Lieutenant Koop stated,

"Well, well, look at this. He's finally out of Segregation. I bet the next time I tell him to shut the fuck up, he will do as I tell him to do." As the Lieutenant talked directly to the unit Sgt, he stated, "You know what we did to him? We beat that little fucker up so he would shut up about his property."

My gut instinct made me turn around in my chair so quick to express my inner parent on this guy who just admitted he beat this kid up in the elevator with his hands cuffed behind his back. I stated,

"Aren't you so proud of yourself for beating that kid up, and you broke his jaw on both sides! Aren't you so proud of yourself?"

Dean got up and had the sergeant open the door to let her out on the pod.

I was always told by the staff, even a Captain, that all inmates lie. I know that is not true and I believed Mr. Peabody. After the Lieutenant left the unit, I got a grievance report and gave it to Mr. Peabody and told him he needed to get a lawyer. This was pure inmate abuse. I would not allow someone to do that to my child or anyone else's child, for that matter. My own incident report disappeared about the Lieutenant admitting he beat this kid up. I was never called down to the captain's office, nor was it ever spoken about again.

In Volume 2, you will delve deeper into Officer Purtue's remarkable journey—a story of resilience forged in the crucible of dysfunction and poverty. From a homeless teen mother and high school dropout to a survivor of daily beatings in a family riddled with domestic violence, her early life was a cycle of learned behaviors that led her to seek out the same toxic environments in adulthood. Violence begets violence, and trauma builds upon trauma.

Her story continues with near-death experiences, crippling anxiety, addiction, homelessness, and relentless dysfunction. The question looms: How much can one person endure? Yet, within this darkness lies a journey of recognition, healing, and moving forward.

This volume also provides a raw, unflinching look into the Department of Corrections—a world rife with toxic work environments, apathetic leadership, and systemic failures that erode professionalism and self-care. These conditions not only harm the individuals who serve within the system but also undermine the critical mission of healing those they are entrusted to rehabilitate.

Through it all, Officer Purtue's unwavering resolve to make a difference shines. Her journey reveals the personal and professional challenges of working within a broken system while offering hope, insight, and a call to action.

Volume 2 promises to uncover more stories and truths that will surprise and enlighten readers, painting a vivid picture of survival, redemption, and the fight for meaningful change.

XXXXXXXXXXXXX

Made in the USA
Monee, IL
12 March 2025

13917789R00069